Success in Spelling.
A Study of the factors affecting improvement in Spelling in the junior school

Margaret L. Peters

Cambridge Institute of Education
Shaftesbury Road, Cambridge
1970

Printed in England by Henry Burt & Son Ltd, Kempston, Bedford

SBN: 9500202 3 0

Contents

Preface

This is an enquiry into the factors which influence attainment and progress in spelling in children aged nine to eleven. A distinction is made between the molar and the molecular approaches, the molar being the study of attainment and improvement in spelling in relation to major child and teaching variables, the molecular being the detailed breakdown of what is involved in learning to spell. The main body of the monograph is concerned with the molar approach.

In order to investigate child and teaching variables, a survey was made of the spelling attainment and progress of a complete L.E.A. age-group of 846 children, and of their 65 teachers' attitudes and behaviour through the final two primary school years. To assess the relative strengths of variables, correlational and other analyses were performed. Independent variables included intrinsic characteristics of children, family, home and school contributions, teachers' attitudes to priorities in children's writing, methodology, testing, marking, correction exacting, and time spent on various aspects of spelling teaching and creative writing.

The analyses suggest that actual spelling *ability* can be most strongly predicted by verbal intelligence and good visual perception together with care, and speed in writing, a rule-following approach and generalizing ability, with some slight contribution from socio-economic status, and family order and size. In the case of *progress* in spelling, however, these last three variables were found to be only slightly predictive. Progress seems to depend much more on other variables. Analysis of the teacher variable shows quite clearly the importance of the teacher's skill, and particularly of the value of teaching lists of words directly related to children's writing needs. A separate investigation is reported which shows the effect of different methods of teaching reading on spelling.

The investigation makes clear that spelling is a skill acquired by children linguistically favoured, but that linguistically deprived children can and do acquire the skill by rational, systematic teaching.

The monograph ends with a tentative examination of the nature of spelling as a skill.

Acknowledgements

This piece of research was, in its original form, accepted as a Ph.D. thesis in the University of London. For the facilities and grant which made the research possible, I wish to thank the Director, and the Cambridge Institute of Education, and I acknowledge with gratitude the co-operation of the local authorities, heads and teachers of schools concerned and that of many students and colleagues.

My thanks are particularly due to my supervisor, Professor Thelma Veness, formerly of Birkbeck College, now of the University of London Institute of Education; also to Brian Murphy, Birkbeck College for his invaluable help in computer programming and statistical analysis; and to Professor Brian Lewis formerly of the University of London Institute of Education, now of the Open University, for his generous advice on statistics.

My thanks are also due to Dr. Joyce Morris without whose insistence the research would never have been started, to my former colleague Professor John McLeish, without whose generous support it would probably never have continued, and most of all, to my husband Professor Richard Peters, without whose encouragement it would certainly never have been completed.

I The Problem of Spelling

1. *The Ideological Context*

The present period is one of controversy in education which affects all levels of the educational system. At the primary level the controversy revolves very much round the role of the teacher. Should she be directive or complaisant? Should she concern herself with the teaching of tools or just encourage children to express themselves? How important is content as distinct from creativity?

These are really false dichotomies. For how can children express themselves at all articulately without tools, however rudimentary? And is creativity without any kind of content an intelligible, let alone a desirable ideal? Nevertheless the controversy persists because basically it reflects the clash between the old ideology of the elementary school and that of the child-centred movement. The controversy itself is now very dated—but the ideologies persist in practices, or in the criticism of practices. The teacher, therefore, who has been brought up in the climate of opinion created by the clash of these ideologies, finds that a practice such as the teaching of spelling puts her into an acute conflict state. She is uneasy about teaching spelling because of what she has heard about not being directive from the priests of the child-centred movement; on the other hand she feels that spelling does matter—though she is not quite sure why—and she senses that spelling is not one of those things that can just be picked up from the environment like a cockney accent. Discussion of a particular child's progress rarely concludes without some comment such as 'He has lots of ideas and gets them down; but he can't spell.' Even if a teacher believes that there is a rational case for spelling—e.g. because it helps communication and because it frees children to write fluently without insecurity, there is a further problem about its place in the curriculum and about the methods by means of which it should be taught.

When the writer started her research on spelling she questioned a representative sample of teachers about their attitude to spelling. Statements such as 'I am in a complete state of uncertainty about spelling; please help if you can,' or 'I do not know whether I am right to do no list-learning. Perhaps your tests will give some answer to this,' reveal very well the state of insecurity in which so many teachers find themselves about spelling. But what people say is one thing and what they do is often quite another. Do many teachers in fact teach in a traditional way in spite of their verbal allegiance to another ideology? Bennett (1967) comments that traditional practices in their condensed form may occur more commonly than official curricula and published articles would lead us to suppose. The actual practices of teachers in relation to spelling may diverge from their expressed attitudes.

2. *What is Spelling?*

The confusion in which teachers find themselves about spelling thus reflects in part the more general ideological conflict about the role of the teacher and of content

1

in an educational situation. But there are additional reasons why spelling should be the centre of so much perplexity; for it is not an activity which is altogether straightforward like digging a hole in the ground. If a teacher thinks that spelling must be taught rather than just picked up, she is only at the beginning of her problems. For there are countless forms of activity which constitute 'teaching' which have little else in common except that they are ways of getting others to learn. But there are many forms of learning. Learning to skip is very different from learning to do quadratic equations. Until the teacher is clear about what has to be learnt it will not be obvious what kind of teaching is appropriate. What, then, has to be learnt in spelling?

Obviously learning to spell is not like learning dates or distances. It is not a matter of learning facts. It is usually thought of as a skill. But there are many different kinds of skill. Is it a skill like cooking, where there are rules? Is it like reading, where there is a large element of understanding as well as discriminatory skills? Or is it like rote learning which depends mainly on laws of association such as frequency, rather than on implicit rules? Or is it like swimming, which depends on the integration of motor sub-skills? Unless we know what is involved we do not know what to emphasize in *teaching* or what it is that children may learn to do by themselves in suitably contrived environments.

It would seem that the more complex the skill the greater the cognitive element. In cooking, motor dexterity, rule-following and understanding go hand in hand. In reading, the integration of successive and simultaneous movements, that is successive approximation of sub-skills to the skill as a whole, must coincide with understanding. As understanding increases, however, attention to visuo-motor aspects decreases, and only reappears when, for example, a long unfamiliar word is to be read, and the reader uses phonics as a reserve technique, (MacKinnon 1959) or 'low gear', (Cronbach 1954). Spelling would seem to be this kind of skill. Schonell's classic analysis of spelling as a 'complex sensory motor process the efficiency of which is based on repeated motor reactions to sensory stimuli' (Schonell 1942) suggests clearly that spelling is a skill more like reading than like cookery or rote-learning. Yet there are fundamental differences between the skills of reading and spelling. For example, in reading discriminatory skills coincide with understanding, but emphasis on these is reduced until the competent reader not only does not fixate letters, but not even words, and there is no conscious awareness of component units. In spelling, understanding of a word or phrase necessarily precedes the writing of it. And before the 'automatic, predictable, infallible' spelling of which Schonell spoke is achieved, there may be a conscious deliberation in selection of the correct alternative, and much writing practice. Ambivalent attitudes on the part of teachers may indeed depend on what kind of a skill spelling is, since teachers do not know what kind of thing it is they should be teaching even if they think they ought to be teaching it.

3. *The Molar and the Molecular approach to Spelling*

In drawing attention to the confusion in which teachers find themselves about spelling, a distinction has been drawn between factors which derive from the ideology of teachers as reflected in their practices and factors deriving from the actual com-

2

plexity of spelling as a skill which has to be learnt. This distinction suggests that, if anyone, such as the writer, is interested in attempting to understand the factors on which improvement in spelling depends this could be studied in a gross or molar way by attempting to correlate improvement in spelling with factors such as teachers' attitudes and behaviour and the methods which they use, or it could be studied in a more refined or molecular way by breaking down the components of spelling as a skill and constructing experimental teaching situations in which some factors rather than others in this molecular analysis were varied.

The writer has chosen the first of these two alternatives in the study of spelling although it may be that the second alternative is likely to yield more precise and important results in the long run. The choice of the first alternative was determined partly by the fact that there is, as yet, no satisfactory molecular type of analysis of spelling as a skill. The writer hopes, however, that some of the findings of the molar approach may help to reveal more clearly the general features of such a refined analysis and thus pave the way for further studies at the molecular level.

There are many ways of breaking down the molar variables on which improvement in spelling seems to depend. For the sake of convenience the following crude distinctions have been used for the purpose of this research:

(a) *Child Variables*

Obviously one of the most crucial variables in learning to spell is what the child himself brings to the learning situation. It is, for instance, a reasonable hypothesis, about which the writer has some evidence, that in the case of some children they bring so much with them to the learning situation that neither method nor skill on the part of the teacher is crucial. As one head put it: 'Less able children tend to need "word drill" more than highly intelligent children who can learn to spell quite naturally.' If this is so, if some children acquire the skill, if not 'naturally', yet at an early age without deliberate teaching, what factors in the children have brought this about? What attributes and skills do such children possess and what conditions in the home have contributed to such spelling ability?

(b) *Teaching Variables*

In a recent *Review of Educational Research* (1967) it was noted that one limitation in spelling research has been neglect of the teacher variable. For example, little has been done to investigate the quality of the teacher—e.g. as indexed by teaching grades, etc., or to survey methods actually employed to teach spelling. One of the objectives of the writer's research has been to discover the attitudes of teachers to spelling, how, if at all, they teach it and whether what they omit to do bears any relationship to children's progress. It was expected that teachers' attitudes would determine their teaching behaviour. There would be exposed the dilemma already referred to in which many teachers find themselves in-respect to the teaching of spelling. How teachers teach may depend in part on their attitude to what they are teaching, but it obviously also depends on the quality of the teacher, on his rationality, consistency, and awareness of how a skill is learned. The use of research findings is also relevant in this context. Throughout the study, reference has been made to

3

teaching rather than teacher variables since the latter could well include such aspects as personality, attitudes, or concern with the normative structure of conception of the teacher's role, instead of the particular facet of teaching behaviour to be examined here.

(c) *Influence of Reading Methods on Spelling*

Of general interest in the context of the primary school is the influence of reading methods on spelling. The writer previously conducted an investigation into this question. These findings do not fall neatly into the category of either child or teacher variables, but they are included in this monograph for their obvious interest and relevance.

The plan will therefore be to study
(*a*) Child variables;
(*b*) Teaching variables;
(*c*) The influence of reading methods.

The research conducted will be summarized and certain tentative conclusions formulated on the basis of this research. There will then be a final chapter in which some implications for molecular study of spelling will be extracted from this research at the molar level.

It is to be emphasized that in the case of spelling the study of teaching and child variables are being surveyed in relation to a skill that is highly resistant to analysis. Bennett points out at the end of a critical review of the contribution of linguistics to spelling (Bennett 1967): 'The stream of optimistic articles which have recently appeared in American journals has so far added little to our knowledge of the subject.' This kind of criticism has been taken account of in this research; for the main part of the study is to show that the kind of thing that has to be learned in spelling explains in part the results of the molar findings—e.g. that intelligent children learn to spell without difficulty whereas dull children need considerable systematized instruction, that spelling ability depends very largely on visual perception of word structure, and that teachers who are rational and consistent in their approach bring about progress in the children whom they teach. It is to be hoped that this approach to the learning of a particular skill, namely spelling, will be of interest not only in its own right but also in the more general context of teaching and learning and the relationship between them.

4

II Previous Research

Table 1 *Flow Chart of Theoretical Aspects of the Subject*

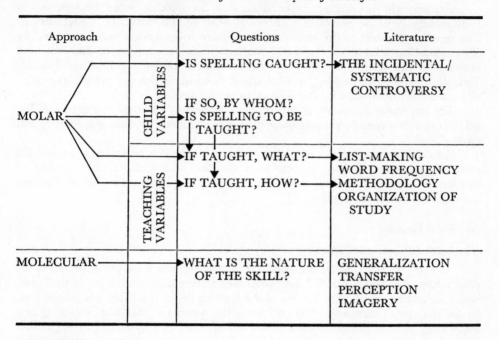

Approach		Questions	Literature
MOLAR	CHILD VARIABLES	IS SPELLING CAUGHT?	THE INCIDENTAL/ SYSTEMATIC CONTROVERSY
		IF SO, BY WHOM? IS SPELLING TO BE TAUGHT?	
	TEACHING VARIABLES	IF TAUGHT, WHAT?	LIST-MAKING WORD FREQUENCY
		IF TAUGHT, HOW?	METHODOLOGY ORGANIZATION OF STUDY
MOLECULAR		WHAT IS THE NATURE OF THE SKILL?	GENERALIZATION TRANSFER PERCEPTION IMAGERY

Molar Approach

Of the two approaches to the problem of spelling, the molar and the molecular, it is the former that is being used in this survey, and it is the questions that prompt this approach, which have prompted much of the research on spelling pursued in the past. The survey was intended in the first place to examine the extent to which spelling was caught, and to identify children to whom it had to *be taught*. If taught the question was 'What was being taught? And how was it being taught?' Apart from this last question, these are areas of concern reflecting the main streams of research into spelling that have been navigated in the last seventy years. They are empirically based and highly controversial. Most of the research so far pursued has been in relation to the incidental/systematic controversy, and to list making, work frequency and methodology.

As the gross findings of the study of the child variable indicated, surprisingly clearly, the pattern of *which* children 'caught' the skill and which children needed to be taught, it is the literature in the incidental/systematic controversy that is most

5

relevant here. In order to fit this specific research into spelling under the headings of the present investigation, the incidental/systematic controversy will therefore be classified under CHILD VARIABLES. The original intention had been to include a review of literature relating to *other* child variables such as left-handedness, visual and auditory defect, etc. As, however, the research showed these to be of little importance, it was decided to omit reference to this body of literature which seems of little relevance to spelling.

Similarly the previous research done into list making, word frequency and methodology, will be classified under the heading TEACHING VARIABLES. The research relevant to the section of the present investigation under the heading *Child Variables*, relates to the incidental/systematic controversy. The research relevant to the section of the present investigation under the heading *Teaching Variables*, relates to list making, word frequency and methodology, (which is specifically concerned with what is often known as generalization).

The molecular approach recalls tenuous attempts to analyse the nature of the skill. It is highly speculative and there is little in the literature that is specific to this particular skill.

Before proceeding to the reporting of the research, it is necessary to review the relevant literature. As can be seen from the flow chart above, the problem of incidental learning in spelling is fundamental to the spelling survey whose findings are reported in this monograph.

A. *Child Variables*

The Incidental/Systematic Controversy

As early as 1897, when the teaching of spelling was a universal practice, the possibilities of its being 'caught' were beginning to be considered. Rice, in that year, wrote an article called, 'The futility of the spelling grind', and this was followed up by for example, Cornman (1902) criticizing the systematic teaching of spelling and suggesting, with statistical evidence, that spelling could be approached through other activities such as written work and reading. Though the possibility of spelling being 'caught' rather than 'taught' was challenged soon after by Wallin (1910) with further statistical evidence in favour of the 'taught' rather than 'caught' school, the controversy had come to stay, simmering in America, but not boiling until the second quarter of the century with Grace Fernald, who in *Remedial Techniques in the Basic School Subjects* (1943,206) emphasized that 'the most satisfactory spelling vocabulary is that supplied by the child himself' in the course of his own expression. Kyte (1948) supported this view with reservations, advocating the withdrawal of good spellers from formal spelling lessons. Even these, he said, would need to be regularly tested, to ensure that they maintained their competence.

Meanwhile in 1941 in England, Nisbet had mitigated the extremism of Fernald by pointing out that children are likely to 'catch' only one new word out of every twenty-five they read. With older people who are unsophisticated readers, this may also be true, but with serious, slower, more focussed readers such as students, the gain in spelling ability from mere reading could be expected to be greater, particularly in more technical words that may be new to the student, who might pick up the spelling from the significant etymology of the word. Gilbert (1935) found that college students' spelling certainly improved as they read, the extent of the improvement depending on the type of reading and the reader's purpose. Words that had been recently brought to their attention were 'caught' more effectively than words encountered more remotely, and good spellers learned more words than poor spellers.

The role of incidental learning had become respectable. 'Incidental learning is indirect learning,' wrote Hildreth (1956,33), 'which takes place when the learner's attention is centred not in improving the skill in question, but on some other objective ...' and qualified this a moment later with, 'Teachers should not think of incidental learning and integrated teaching as excluding systematic well organized drill. Rather from the child's attempts to write will come evidence of his need for systematic word study.' So not only the spelling will be 'caught', but the need to learn to spell also.

From the evidence so far, then, it looks as if:

(a) Not all children need formal spelling lessons, though the competence of any such children in spelling must be regularly tested. (Kyte, 1948)

(b) Children are likely to learn how to spell (catch) only about 4% of the words they read. (Nisbet, 1941)

(c) 'Catching' words incidentally seems to occur when children's attention is centred on some object other than improving the skill itself. (Hildreth, 1956)

(d) The casual experience of words in reading lessons is, in the case of young and backward children, insufficient for recording permanent impressions. (Schonell, 1942)

(e) College students' spelling improves by reading, particularly of words brought to their attention. Better spellers learn more new words through reading than poor spellers. (Gilbert, 1935)

Obviously the more competent the reader, the greater resources for spelling reference. As Mackay and Thompson (1968, 66) point out, 'The fluent reader has an internalized model of the orthography, although he is unlikely to be able to say what this model looks like.' But this is not to say that the model provides a sufficient condition for spelling competence. The model may be internalized, without the strategies for utilizing this being exploited.

There is then some evidence as to who acquires the skill incidentally and in what circumstances. The assumption has hitherto been that unless spelling *is* 'caught' in the process of reading, it has to be 'taught' via 'useful' lists. It is with such lists that the second main stream of research has been concerned.

B. *Teaching Variables*

1. *Listmaking and Word Frequency*

Long before the incidental learning controversy teachers were concerned with what words children should learn and they were making word lists to this end. One dated 1882, but found in a primary school cupboard in the 1950's, includes in one lesson the words, 'bissextile', 'decennial', 'chimerical', and 'chalybeate'! Such lists

7

are obviously not derived from children's language either spoken or written. Indeed it was not until 1911 that words ceased to be selected arbitrarily and were selected on the basis of the frequency with which they occurred. In that year Eldridge recorded the 60,000 most common English words from newspapers. In the next few years counts were made particularly of the spelling vocabulary of personal and business letters (Ayres, 1913) because here spelling deficiency was most embarrassingly revealed. The following year the first list derived from children's writing (Cook and O'Shea, 1914) appeared. This has been succeeded through the years by many counts taken from children's writing of compositions and letters, culminating in the recent word counts of children's writing by Edwards and Gibbons in their Leicestershire Vocabulary Survey which, though designed to help writers and publishers of books for the youngest readers, is an indication of the words children write, not necessarily what they want to write.

Since counts of words used by children in their own writing are the most real evidence of what children want to write, it is obviously on these that the spelling lists should be based. Not many, however, are based directly on children's writing. One of the most extensive and thorough is that by Rinsland (1945), who examined and graded more than six million words in 100,000 scripts of children, from 416 American cities. The resulting spelling list contained only words appearing more than three times in any one grade. This list was further graded by Hildreth (1953) who noted how words became so highly specialized after the first 2,000 or so that it was difficult to determine which to include in primary school spelling lists. Johnson's list (1950) from children's writing was confined to the hundred words he found that children in their writing were most likely to mis-spell. In 1955, the Scottish Council for Research in Education took a much more positive line by producing a spelling vocabulary, derived from a count of the words in 70,000 compositions written freely by 7–12 year-old pupils in Scottish schools, on topics selected to suit their interests.

Many lists, however, have been prepared, often subjectively, from other sources, often remote from children's writing needs, from e.g. adults' correspondence or adults' reading material, as was the famous 30,000 word list of Thorndike and Lorge (1944). To do this is to teach children to spell words that adults, not they themselves, write. No wonder Fernald wrote 'Formal word lists will always fail to supply the particular word a person should learn at a particular time' (1943, 210). Words which children are learning from derived lists may well be the words they will not need till they themselves are adult and writing formal letters; for it has been found that there is little in common between the vocabulary of children's writing and that of adults' formal literary writing. Hildreth confirmed earlier findings that derived spelling word lists were very different in content from the words used in children's writing. She also found that word forms that children use may be different from the forms appearing in derived lists e.g. children make more frequent use of the past tense and of the plural form than the present tense and singular form that appear in the lists.

If a list is derived it is important to know its source. Apart from those already mentioned as having stemmed from word counts of children's writing, most spelling lists have been derived from word counts, particularly from Thorndike's. Washburne's spelling curriculum (1923) was based partly on Thorndike's lists, though in part on adult correspondence and children's compositions. Breed (1930) answered, 'What words should children be taught to spell?' from sixteen different sources, eleven of which were adult. Even Schonell's familiar 'Essential Spelling List' (1932), the one most widely used in English schools, is a subjective list derived from Horn (adults' writing, 1926) and Thorndike (adults' reading material, 1921), though here there is an empirically based relationship with well standardized norms of spelling ability, i.e. with what children can, not necessarily with what they want to spell.

Gates' (1937) list was derived from a count of words in twenty-five spelling books used in American schools. Bixler (1940) produced a standard spelling scale from eight sources and thus to the popular *Keywords to Literacy* (1962), a derived list, but one intended as a minimum sight vocabulary to be used in the teaching of reading and not primarily intended as a spelling list.

From such lists, the Bureau of Curriculum Research of the Board of Education in the City of New York compiled a list of 5,000 words graded into ten frequency levels. From this State list, the New Zealand Council of Educational Research list of 2,700 words was originally derived (1960). But this was only a starting point. This list was widely examined by inspectors, college lecturers and teachers, and checked against a number of well-known derived lists as well as word counts of New Zealand children's writing. By so checking, the faults and omissions of a derived list have been ironed out and the resulting list is almost certainly the most adequate in use today.

2. *Methodology*

(i) *Lists without Prescribed Techniques*

Many spelling books have been produced with lists devised in various ways, but few until recently said much about how to set about learning. Students presented with nonsense words to learn to spell, soon find it necessary to evolve an efficient method. Most students depend on associative clues and mnemonics; rarely do they depend on rote learning. Must children, inexperienced in organization of material to be learned and unaware of the laws of learning, be expected to evolve by trial and error an economical method of learning spelling lists?

Learning to spell, without being given instructions as to how to learn, leads to haphazard techniques which may well be inappropriate to a particular child's idiosyncrasies of perception and imagery. It may, for example, lead children to spell 'alphabetically'. This is a time-honoured method, but it involves an unnecessarily complicated sequence of events. The child learns the word by reading it and repeating the alphabetic names of the letters. He writes it by first saying the name of each letter in turn and writing it before reading the completed word. He is using two distinct letter attributes, name and power (sound). One does not immediately evoke the other. If we hear a word spelt by alphabetic names, the word is not immediately meaningful. Nor is it inevitably, if the word is spelt by the sounds of the language, since sounds in themselves have only value in relation to their immediate environment. But it is more immediately meaningful than if spelt by alphabetic names. The individual, hearing the sequence of sounds, adapts the sounds to fit the letter environment, and, with anticipation of sequence, completes the word. Recitation of letter

'names' even more than recitation of 'sounds' is only one example of the precarious-
ness of leaving children uninstructed to learn to spell by trial and error.

Fulton pointed out in 1914, in the days when spelling lists of dubious origin and
derivation abounded, that pupils following a systematic method make much greater
progress and retain their learning better than those given no directions for learning to
spell. Twenty years later Alice Watson (1935) was recommending that children
should be taught to master efficient techniques for self-teaching. Only too often
children, given a list without a method, read over the list rapidly or recite the names
of the letters, names that have no immediate relation to the overall sound of the
word. A somewhat more sophisticated way of learning is to learn syllabically, sound-
ing the syllables one by one. But to rely wholly on auditory memory is to put oneself
in a position of uncertainty when faced with the alternatives presented by even
grapho-phonemically regular words, dependent entirely on a method that breaks
down just when it is most needed. Unsupported by other sensory inroads, this is a
precarious means to spelling. *see Schonell (1948, pp 277-278).*

Schonell (1942), of course, pointed out that the visual, auditory and articulatory
elements must be 'firmly cemented by writing'. For by writing the attention is
focussed and 'helps to bridge the gap between visual and auditory symbols by successive production of the constituent parts of the visual form'. This writing which
gives children the 'feel' of the word is vital to correct spelling. As children progress
they become less and less aware of the visual, auditory, and articulatory elements,
until they achieve the machine-like movement where, as they write, the initial letter
initiates the muscular contraction stimulating the second letter in a chain-like series,
a chain reaction supplying the whole word. There is such a moment in learning to
type when, instead of typing letter by letter, the student suddenly in one sweep
produces a word. T-h-e is produced in one satisying, complete unalterable movement. The first letter, t, triggers off the h, the h, the e, and if the typist images the
word it may well be in muscular contractions in the three fingers involved.

Repeated writing, however much it bridges the gap between visual and auditory
symbols, involves auditory and articulatory elements only implicitly. Schonell spoke
of 'the absolute necessity of emphasizing with backward spellers all means of ingress
in learning words, the visual, the auditory and the kinaesthetic'. A child or adult
may be handicapped by one rather weak sensory mechanism; he may have poor
perceptual grasp of the significance of a word, his imagery may be very one-sided or
he may be distracted by other sensory stimuli. If such a child is bombarded by
several sensory stimuli supporting each other in emphasizing the structure of a word
to remember, he will inevitably attend to and learn the word. And this is what
Fernald suggests (1943): an amalgam of the sensory input. Sight, of course, is being
translated from receptor into effector finger movements and pencil movements, but
it is supplemented by simultaneous oral articulation of the word, the hearing of this
slowly spoken word, together with the tactile sensation as the child traces with his
bare forefinger the word he is learning. Each child possesses an office file and inserts
the word he needs alphabetically, after he has finger-traced it often enough for him
to be able to write it correctly in his composition. Much later we find him, faced
with a new word, finger-tracing unobtrusively on the desk or on his knee! Often the
more sophisticated learner of spelling not only articulates the word subvocally as he

writes, but makes slight head or finger movements, long after he has abandoned a finger-tracing technique, an overt sign of the retention of the oral and kinaesthetic imagery he initiated when learning by finger-tracing. All possible perceptual channels are left open. Children can learn, in spite of their individual differences, without recourse to complicated and tedious investigation by the teacher to find the best method for any particular child to pursue.

The Gates-Russell diagnostic test (1940) is one such elaborate and lengthy type of investigation. As part of a battery of tests (criticized by Spache, 1953, 201, for the lack of a 'critical analysis of validity and reliability') it is unique in that it sets out to reveal the most congenial method a particular child employs in spelling with a view to exploiting the child's habits, strengths and facility. 'Spelling disability', they write (p. 41), 'is usually a highly individual matter', and they are eclectic in their approach to the remedial teaching of spelling. They advocate individual and independent methods of word-study (attention to hard spots, pointing out familiar word forms in longer words, syllabizing, visualizing, hearing, pronouncing the word, spelling it orally, and writing it) and this repeatedly in different situations. They stress the motivational aspect, changed attitudes to spelling, and changed habits, for example, of verifying doubtful words. In such an 'unphonetic language as English' they point out 'the importance of good visual techniques'. Children should work on their own errors as well as on lists; and devices unrelated to spelling are of less use than intrinsic functional practice materials, emphasizing context spelling rather than words in isolation.

This, though an eclectic programme for individuals, is all-embracing since it includes both the multi-sensory approach as advocated by Fernald for universal use and the word-study approach.

A number of spelling books have been published in the last few years fulfilling various functions. Some still present lists of words to be learned without any indication of how to learn. In some, such as *Spelling* by John Smith (1961), this is deliberate. Words are grouped according to structure, and children find the word that fits the definition and write it down, presumably copying it, but the internal structure will have been noted. The children are not told how to learn these, in fact they are not told to learn them at all. Their object is the search for a word, and it is very probable that, provided, as in this case, attention is centred on the structure of a word, spelling is more easily acquired when the object is something other than just learning to spell. After all, the motivation is stronger in searching for a word and completing a whole.

(ii)   *Lists with Suggested Techniques*

The spelling lists with the most explicit technical instructions as to how to learn are those in the *Alphabetical Spelling List* prepared and published by the New Zealand Council for Educational Research. The first English edition was published in 1963. It consists of an alphabetical list of words, as has already been described, derived from the New York State list.

The frequency levels of the chosen words are indicated for each of the words, so that children can see for themselves how relatively probable it is that the words they are learning will be needed by them. This at once indicates the degree of

11

autonomy expected of the children in this field. A child is expected to compile a personal learning list and if words entered are from a lower level than his current working level, these should be underlined, thus providing automatic revision. 'The child', says Arvidson (1963, 20), 'should be encouraged to adopt a particularly determined attitude towards words that persistently give him trouble.' Again the onus is on the child in this learning situation.

The dictionary form of the spelling list demands dictionary skills. The child must isolate the first and later the second and third letters of a word, have some idea of the part of the dictionary to open, and range forward and backward till the word is found. When it is found, specific instructions are given to copy the word. In the later learning period, the child is given instructions as to how to learn to spell, by writing, looking, saying, listening, saying again, finger-tracing on the desk and saying as he writes. He is instructed to cover and write from memory with his finger, and later to write with a pencil and check.

These are specific instructions, for a systematic procedure. It is assumed that the children work autonomously, independently, and responsibly. They are instructions to children to use a number of 'perceptual paths into the memory', visual, auditory, kinaesthetic, followed by testing, overlearning and revision.

Arvidson reminds us of individual differences in learning methods and recommends that the weaker spellers should be studied and helped to find their best technique. But instructions accompanying the word lists are systematic generalized instructions for class use.

(iii) *Organization of Study*

Another organizational factor that has repeatedly appeared in research writings involves good techniques of study. In two investigations Gilbert (1932 a and b) showed that 'limiting study time may work to the advantage of the learner.' In investigations into the effects of teaching spelling through insistence on speed and accuracy of visual perception, Gilbert and Gilbert (1942) concluded that the most important task for the teacher was the proper marshalling of effort. Good techniques of study should involve finding the optimum study rate of pupils. Time spent on visual examination of the word should be limited, since they found that judicious training could effect an increase in rate and efficiency, and improve perceptual habits. They were quite clear that the practice of assigning words to be studied for an unlimited period was unprofitable and undesirable. Spelling should be taught, definite instructions being given as to how to learn, and should proceed as quickly as possible.

In a study of eye-movements, Gilbert (1932 b) described one of the most efficient twelve year old spellers, who, in the pre-test wrote 'definitely' as 'definitly'. In the subsequent learning of its spelling, however, her eye movement record showed that she paid very little attention to the 'e' she had previously omitted. Another twelve year old, in learning to spell the word ' questionnaire' spent most of the learning period on the study of the word 'question' which she had spelled correctly in the pre-test. In spite of 'knowing' the word, she studied it! It is as long ago as 1919 that Horn advised us to test all words before teaching. It was to avoid this kind of wasted time and effort in unnecessary learning that test-study rather than study-test methods were evolved. (Fitzgerald, 1953). Freyberg (1960) advocates a positive approach to the teaching of spelling, a systematic approach demanding set word-study periods and autonomy of learning.

Before summarizing the task of the teacher in establishing the best conditions under which children will learn to spell competently, let us look back half a century to Horn (1919) and Gill (1912) who put a case for systematic instruction in spelling. 'There is no short cut to spelling,' Horn said and his five rules for teaching spelling are apposite today.

Rules

1. Test all words before teaching.
2. Let each child work only on the words difficult for him and provide him with a definite method of learning them.
3. Provide for rigorous reviews.
4. Show the pupil his progress daily, weekly, monthly and yearly.
5. Keep up his interest.

This puts us well and truly on the systematic side of the incidental/systematic controversy, where we began.

But still we are dealing with organization of teaching and not with the actual learning of the skill. Indeed this is what the *molecular* approach is concerned with.

C. *Molecular Approach*

Unless one knows the nature of the skill, i.e. what one is trying to teach, it would seem pointless to discuss methodology, and particularly organization. Even the vexed question of incidental learning versus systematic teaching would seem irrelevant unless one knew what it was one was trying to teach. Yet this is what has happened in the literature, mainly because spelling has not been seen as a skill very different from reading. Encoding was not seen to be very different from decoding. It is, in fact, one of the intentions of the writer to show that the two are very different kinds of skills.

The contributions, in the literature, to analysis of the skill have been in the area of what has come to be called 'generalization'.

Generalization

So far discussion has centred on the methodology of list-learning i.e. of learning each word separately, on the assumption that English spelling is so irregular that no rules can be formulated to reduce the burden of words to be learned. Now rules can be of several kinds:

1. Generalization of phoneme/grapheme correspondence, which is a necessary initial stage in learning to spell, but which involves, as will be later demonstrated, some serious and, because of the nature of the language, inevitable difficulties.
2. Explicit, formulated rules.
3. Generalization of a completely different kind, in the learning, not of phoneme/grapheme correspondence or formulated rules or principles, but in the learning of serial probability.

13

1. *Generalization of Phoneme/Grapheme Correspondence*

For this to occur universally, the language would have to be completely regular, which English is manifestly *not*. Indeed, the extent to which English is irregular has been the prime determinant of whether generalization in rule-forming can occur. The criteria must first be listed—

(i) *Criteria*

Criteria of regularity vary from one investigation to another. The commonest criterion is 'phonetic regularity'. The word 'phonetic' is used here incorrectly, since 'phonetics' are concerned with spoken not written language, and in the following 'criteria', for the words 'phonetic regularity', there should be substituted some such phrase as 'one to one correspondence of phoneme-grapheme', or Gibson's (1965, 1071) more precise definition of spelling pattern 'a cluster of graphemes in a given environment which has an invariant pronunciation according to the rules of English'. Before the days of such precise terminology, investigators had been using these same criteria however. In 1953 Hanna and Moore, analysed the incidence of 'phonetic units in children's speech and writing'. Groff (1961) looking at the New Iowa Spelling Scale (1954) which had been constructed from the written communications of adults and children assessed 'words that were not entirely phonetic.' Hildreth (1962) examined the number of different sounds given to the same letter or letter combination, the number of written combinations that can evoke one sound and the number of words containing silent letters, and calls her criterion 'regular sounded elements'.

(ii) *New Methods of Establishing Criteria*

In 1964 a Swedish investigation led by Ahlstrom, revealed in factor analysis, an 'auditory discrimination factor' involving prediction of pronunciation from a written nonsense word and prediction of spelling from a spoken nonsense word—a factor the Swedes termed 'knowledge of spelling rules'. This will be discussed later—but it is relevant here since, simultaneously, there was an investigation by the use of computers, into identification of sound-letter correspondence and the extent to which prediction of spelling of words according to phonetic rules was possible. (Lester, 1964; Hodges and Rudorf, 1965). This kind of thing was seen as a way in to 'programming the spelling curriculum' (Hanna and Hanna, 1965). Even so, such analyses are looked on with suspicion by Bennett (1967, 72) who speculates whether 'useful sets of generalizations even when identified, can be effectively utilized in teaching and if so, how?' And Mackay and Thompson (1968) look dubiously at the emphasis on sound-symbol correspondence as 'part of our common heritage of folk linguistics'!

2. *Explicit, Formulated Rules*

Such generalizations from regular phoneme-grapheme correspondence must be distinguished from the more usual concept of 'rules' which have long been accepted as one way into spelling. These are rules which come mainly from teachers' own experience, though a few from textbooks, where the great difficulty is in the wording of the rules, e.g. 'monosyllables and words of more than one syllable with the accent on the last syllable which end in a single consonant preceded by a single vowel double the final consonant when adding a suffix beginning with a vowel.' This is the first of four rules framed by Wheat (1932, 700) and said to cover 23% of the words in the vocabulary he analysed. The length and technicality of such rules are frightening, yet we are reminded that by the time the child needs to spell untaught words, he can comprehend and use such rules. This is very questionable since use of technical terms, e.g. noun, plural, singular, etc., presupposes a conceptual level far in advance of the *use* of nouns, plurals, singulars.

It is generally agreed that:
(*a*) The rule must apply to a large number of words.
(*b*) It must have few exceptions.
(*c*) The statement of the rules must be simple and easily comprehended while being sufficiently exact to cover only the appropriate words.

'Before a new rule is introduced,' writes McLeod (1961, 130) 'the following should be borne in mind. Knowledge of a rule serves no useful purpose unless it covers a number of words which might reasonably be expected to be already in the children's spelling vocabulary and embraces also other words likely to be needed which the children may spell by generalization.' No wonder Vallins (1965, 5) writes 'There are no reliable rules, and even the guiding principles, of which there are more than we imagine, are apt sometimes to fail and mislead both ear and eye.' McLeod's own research showed that presenting each word separately was a better method than teaching words with the aid of such spelling rules where applicable. As Foran (1934) said, 'If a rule involves unfamiliar terms, it may become a major difficulty in itself and contribute nothing to spelling.'

So neither 'useful sets of generalizations', nor explicit formulated rules, are thought to be promising inroads into spelling. Nor do they contribute much to an analysis of the nature of the skill, an analysis which is the objective of the molecular approach.

3. *Generalization through Knowledge of Serial Probability*

We are told that 70% (Groff, 1961) to 85% (Hildreth, 1956) of words in English are 'regular' and this latter percentage is confirmed by Venezsky and Lester (1964). Now the problem is not only with what has been shown to be the 15 to 30% of irregular words but with the 70 to 85% of so-called regular words, words which can have quite reasonable alternatives, e.g. 'great' could reasonably be written 'grate' or 'grait'. The question fundamental to an analysis of the spelling skill is: What determines the right selection from the numerous possible alternatives? The word 'Circumference' Horn claimed, 'could be spelled in 396, 900, 000 ways by using the spellings of identical or similar sounds in words likely to be known to a sixth-grade child.' (1929, 49).

In the analysis of errors in this survey, the writer examined those which were reasonable alternatives, and the criterion of this was 'sequences according to spelling precedent'. Of 967 ten year olds attempting the word 'saucer', for example, 462 children wrote it successfully. The remaining 505 offered between them 209 alternative spellings.* If they had been presented with the word 'saucer' to read, it would have been read correctly according to recent norms (Andrews, 1964) of Schonell's Graded Word Reading Test by 71% of eight year olds, and this in a word reading test where the words are divorced from context. Asked to write it, only 47% of ten year olds were able to write it correctly. In reading, the grapheme is decoded by the child into predictable phonemes. In spelling, the child is encoding a known sound into one of several alternative graphemes. The grapheme selected will approximate closely to, or remotely from, spelling precedent according to how familiar the child is with the kind of letter sequences that occur in his own language. Some of these sequences occur frequently, some seldom. The probability of any sequence occurring is calculable, and as these depart from close approximation to English so the ease of perceptual recognition of these words is reduced. Wallach (1963) presented good and poor spellers with tachistoscopically exposed nonsense words that closely resemble English, and random nonsense words. For random words there was very little difference between good and poor spellers, but good spellers were found to recognize nonsense words resembling English much more readily than poor spellers. The good spellers had learned a general coding system based on the probabilities of letters occurring in certain sequences in English.

This is the case in any language, though there is no transfer from one language to another because the spelling conventions of one language are quite different from the spelling conventions of another. Bruner (1953) quotes an experiment he conducted with Harcourt at an international seminar on the ability to reproduce random strings of letters and nonsense words approximating closely to various languages. There was no difference in ability to handle random strings, but a real difference in ability, favouring one's mother tongue, in reproducing nonsense in one's own language. It is easy to place such nonsense words as MJOLKKOR, KLOOK, GERLANCH, OTIVANCHE, TRIANODE, FATTALONI, etc. As Bruner says, 'When one learns a language one learns a coding system that goes beyond words.'

(i) *Transfer of Training*

Thus spelling achievement, within a particular language, can be assumed to depend on transfer of training, since familiarity is a powerful determinant of ease of perceptual recognition when a word is exposed for a brief period of time (Howes and Solomon, 1951). Wallach (1963) concludes that good spellers show much more transfer than poor spellers whether the basis for this transfer rests on the learning of the sequential probability of letters or phonetic generalization or both. For the present the query must be left open. In the light of examination of the probability of alternative spellings being produced it may be made clearer which kind of generalization is the more potent.

(ii) *Visual Perception of Word Form*

Knowledge of serial probability necessarily depends on visual perception of word form, which can either be acquired subconsciously and peripherally or by teacher direction.

* See Appendix C(i).

16

This knowledge of serial probability is not only a sub-skill essential to the encoding skill of spelling, but it can be seen in proof-reading. Here proofs are scanned and unfamiliar letter sequences spot-lighted. The fact that training in proof reading leads to gain in spelling ability (Goss cit. De Boer, 1961) supports the claim that visual perception of word form, even though peripheral, is a most important element in the acquisition of knowledge of letter sequences. Though Mason (1961) found that nonsense syllables proved as effective as real words for developing the visual discrimination necessary to improve spelling, the closer the approximation of these nonsense syllables to English structure the more knowledge of serial probability is acquired simultaneously with visual discrimination (Wallach, 1963).

It is appropriate here to put forward what is known about the peripheral and central aspects of visual perception of word form.

(a) *Peripheral*

In the light of emphasis placed throughout this monograph on the importance of looking, it might be expected that children with poor sight might be handicapped in spelling. Apart from the inevitable handicaps and their repercussions on spelling experienced by the partially sighted, children who have to wear glasses and yet are within the range of normality, spell as well as those who do not. It is not acuity of vision that distinguishes the good spellers from the bad (Russell, 1937).

It is possible that if the visual field is limited for some reason, the child, like a horse in blinkers, sees only a small area at a time. This could explain the smaller visual memory span often found in poor spellers (Spache, 1940 c). It does not look, however, as if the acuity of vision, which makes a child able to discriminate visually between letters, is a cause of inability to spell as much as it is an earlier cause of inability to read. Even in reading, isolated sensory deficiencies have hardly ever been shown to be insurmountable handicaps (Fendrick, 1935).

With normal children spelling ability is not so much affected by slight peripheral disabilities as by central difficulties (Hartmann, 1931).

(b) *Central*

It is important at the outset to distinguish between neural impairment which is very readily confused with sensory disability. The child's ears and eyes may be efficient but the child still cannot hear or see. What looks like perceptual disability may of course be habitual lack of attention, for severe neural impairment of the kind that would inevitably affect reading and spelling is rare.

There seems to be, however, one aspect of the perceptual process that really does affect spelling. Hartmann (1931) spoke of it as a particular 'form of looking', which was quite distinct from any specific sensory ability or facility in integrating such sensory abilities.

Let us consider what is meant by this particular 'form of looking'. Although the small span of visual apprehension found in poor spellers can be associated with a visual field limited optically, in the retina itself, it is what goes on when a child reproduces a word from a flash card that is interesting in this connection. Good spellers perceive total configurations or, one might say, see the word as a whole more easily than poor spellers (Hartmann, 1931). Now we work on the assumption that

17

perceptual disabilities can be compensated for in training and we know what the more familiar words are, the more likely we are to see them as a whole (Howes and Solomon, 1951). So this may well be a means of training this perception of wholes, by teaching the child to spell words already familiar to him. It is a strong justification for the infant school practice of 'catching words' and of making a start at learning the word as a whole when written in his personal dictionary by the teacher, and not blindly copying. The need to look at words as wholes has been repeatedly observed. As early as 1923, Hilderbrandt suggested that, in learning to spell, it was unwise to lay too much stress on phonic elements, as these might well obstruct the view of the word as a sequence of significant parts or as a whole. Again in 1936 Higley and Higley recommended that, in learning to spell a word, a child should, in the first instance, just look at the word without saying, spelling or writing it, as these intrusions might confuse his learning.

'Looking at a word as a whole' is a vague term which has been heavily and justifiably criticized by supporters of phonic reading schemes (e.g. Diack, 1960). What this phrase means, in terms of spelling needs, is that the word must be reproducible when exposed for a short time on a tachistoscope or a flash card. For this the word must be either familiar (in terms of reading experiences) or short enough to be within the individual's span of apprehension for unconnected elements. The more familiar the word, the longer it can be. Presumably a word that is familiar to a child in the process of his reading, when exposed on a flash card, is not merely reproduced in a memory image, but recognized as in reading and then in recall *built up into its component parts*. The word is not recalled but remade in the light of the child's reading experience with this particular word. It might have been thought that this would not help in dealing with unfamiliar words; hence the preoccupation of teachers with syllabication, with marking hard spots, etc. But reproducing the word correctly, when it is both new and long, depends on first being able to read it, and then in the light of experience with groups of letters that go together (the old 'sequential probability'), being able to reconstruct the word in plausible forms.

If, on the other hand, we do not limit the time of exposure of a word, by tachistoscope or flash card, but give the child time to study a word he is to spell, his eyes move about the word, lighting on different parts for varying lengths of time and going back over parts again. From looking at such eye-movements it is known that good spellers make fewer and shorter fixations than poor spellers, see more of the word at a time, and make fewer regressive movements. Younger and less mature children are also less efficient in eye-movements than older children. (Gilbert and Gilbert, 1942).

Inefficiency of eye-movements is a perceptual habit which is not a cause of but a concomitant of poor spelling. Gilbert (1932 b) put the cause of this in poor study habits, over emphasis and overstudy, thoroughness rather than efficiency. Indeed Gilbert and Gilbert (1942) demonstrated the possibility of decreasing perceptual time while increasing proficiency in both immediate and delayed recall.

(iii) *Imagery*

Recall, whether immediate or delayed, invokes imagery of some kind, and the shorter the exposure and the longer the sequence exposed, the more the individual must rely on some form of imagery to reconstitute the sequence. This is what Hebb (1968) terms a 'serial reconstruction'. There is no doubt that imagery is of very great importance in spelling. Short and Grey Walter (1954), and Stewart and Smith (1959) related certain brain rhythms and certain forms of imagery, particularly visual. This may well imply that there is initially an organic structural basis to imagery. Yet it would seem that imagery changes its mode as we develop. This is particularly so in the case of abstract thinkers. It is possible that our preferred form of imagery develops, as we mature, from a more generalized system which may or may not have stronger emphases, visual, auditory, kinaesthetic.

Kuhlman (1960) cit. Bruner (1966) showed that children with high imagery are better than children with low imagery at performing tasks in which they must learn to associate arbitrary verbal labels with pictures, and this is a task very similar to spelling. But Hebb (1968) suggests that the difference between those who have little imagery and those who have much may be not a difference of the mechanism of thinking but a difference in the retrievability of the image. And it has been shown that training can help to retrieve the image in the cause of spelling. Given two weeks' training Radaker (1963) found that after one year the imagery trained groups scored significantly higher on spelling tests than did the control group, showing that visual imagery is successful in improving spelling performance over longer periods of time.

In analysing imagery Hebb (1968) emphasizes the motor-component in imagery as much as in perception. What he calls part-perceptions are punctuated by motor excitatations produced by peripheral stimulation. One of them becomes liminal and the result is eye-movement followed by another part-perception. That imagery is so analagous to perception is highly relevant to spelling. In the first place, as Hebb says, the child cannot read backwards in imagery as quickly as from the printed word. 'There is sequential left to right organization of the parts within the apparently unitary presentation corresponding to the order of presentation in perception as one reads English from left to right,'—and of course imaginal reading is basic to spelling. The incompleteness of such imagery is symptomatic of spelling difficulty. The individual can part-perceive a word and be held up when a new fixation does not produce a clear image. What one has to ask is why the new fixation does not produce an image. Is it because, in earlier perception of the word, attention was not directed to subsequent parts of the word—particularly to what has traditionally been known as 'hard spots', i.e. word sequences with possible and reasonable alternatives? The present investigation would make this a plausible hypothesis, since e.g. rational correction technique which is entirely concerned with attention to hard spots is conducive to good spelling. Secondly attention to serial probability of words, that is, to common sequences perceived peripherally in reading and daily life, facilitates imaging, and particularly what has earlier been termed reconstituting of a word or as Hebb (1968) put it 'sequential integration'.

Summary of what is known about the nature of the skill

Since English spelling is not only irregular but unpredictable even where 'regular', it is impossible to learn to spell every word that might be needed. So competent spelling depends on the ability to generalize, possibly, though not very satisfactorily, from explicit formulated rules, more certainly from having learned the serial probability of letter occurrences. This involves transfer via visual perceptions and recall through imagery.

The gross investigation now to be reported exposes these problems in a molar way by examining the intrinsic characteristics of children who achieve spelling ability with ease, and the conditions, techniques and attitudes in the classroom that are conducive to spelling attainment and progress. It is hoped that from the investigation will emerge a clearer picture of the nature of the skill, which will indicate the field for future investigations.

III The Investigation

Introduction

In the light of previous work, there can now be put forward the hypotheses that are to be examined in this investigation. The hypotheses from which this research sprang were concerned with the nature and strength of intrinsic characteristics in children who achieved success in spelling, and with the effect of the teacher variable on the attainment and progress of children in spelling. There is unquestionably concern about why some children and adults (particularly students) find difficulty in spelling. Does this derive from sensory dysfunction, from lack of attention to words, from faulty perception, from motor inefficiency? Or is it related to socio-economic status or family constitution, or merely the reflection of poorly organized intellectual functioning? But beyond this concern about intrinsic characteristics is considerable uneasiness on the part of teachers as to how, if at all, spelling should be taught. The investigation hence extended to two areas:

A. The Child Variable.
B. The Teaching Variable.

In a large survey of this kind it was anticipated that there might be more interesting, though not necessarily relevant information about the instrinsic characteristics and the effect of the teaching variable than indicated in the hypotheses. The particular hypotheses within the three main hypotheses as put forward in Chapter One can be stated as follows :—

A. *Child Variable*

That effective visual perception and imagery, are conducive to spelling ability.

That ability to generalize from known word sequences is necessary to spelling competence.

That there is a calculable probability of a particular word being spelt correctly, incorrectly but reasonably (that is according to spelling precedent) or incorrectly and unreasonably, at a particular time.

B. *Teaching Variable*

That spelling is a skill which must be learned. That the extent to which it is learned will be determined by the teaching of reading and the teaching of written English as well as by the teaching of spelling.

These hypotheses were to be examined in a survey of the spelling ability of a complete Local Education Authority age-group, throughout the final two primary school years, and of the attitudes and practices of the teachers of these children during these years.

There was one particular hypothesis, that perceptual habits, acquired while being taught to read, affect spelling. This it was impossible to test within the confines of the survey so a separate experiment was set up for this purpose. This research is reported in Chapter Five as its conclusions are relevant to the overall hypothesis that visual perception of word structure determines spelling ability since the method by which children learn to read is a determinant of the modes of visual perception of word structure in the primary school.

Child Variable

(a) *Design*

(i) *Subjects*

The survey was of the whole of the age-group of children born between 1.9.54 and 31.8.55, attending primary schools in one L.E.A. Since children leaving and enrolling at these schools during the last two primary school years had to be excluded, the number in the sample fell from 952 in July 1964, to 855 in July 1965, and to 846 in July 1966. (Table 2). There were 58 more boys than girls. All children absent from school on the days of tests were tested subsequently. All testing, interviewing, presentation of questionnaires, etc., throughout was done by one person, the investigator.

The second year junior school age group was selected for the start of the survey for several reasons. There were two complete years to come in the primary school, and one year before the children were involved in selection for secondary education. There was the longer term prospect of six years longitudinal study of these children. Finally, children mid-way through the primary school are expected to write 'freely' and 'creatively', yet they are not too remote from the disciplines of their reading methods. This was found to be immaterial in the case of the survey, but important in the case of the comparison of the effect on spelling of reading methods.

There were nineteen schools in which the numbers of children in this age-group ranged from 10 to 92 (Mean 50, S.D. 24). Eight of these schools, in size, 10 to 36, were small, single stream schools two of which, a boys' and a girls' school subsequently combined. In the others, various combinations of streaming occur, only one of which is wholly permanently and militantly unstreamed. 70.96% of the children were in a streamed class in their second year, 75.6% in their third year and fourth year.

The 'mean' spelling age (Graded Spelling Test Daniels and Diack) at 9 years was 8.6 years (Mean Raw score 29.755 S.D. 9.353) and at 11 years was 11 (Mean raw score 37.897 S.D. 9.768) but it is only to provide this overall picture of the sample that conversion to 'spelling age' was used. In all other calculations and analyses raw scores were used.

The mean socio-economic status of the schools was 3.066 (S.D. 1.067) and the four schools which geographically and traditionally serve University families were scattered, one above, two at, and one below the mean. Mean S.E.S. grades of schools necessarily exclude the extreme grades 1 and 5 (mid-grades emerging) yet no schools graded 4 or 4.5 for mean school S.E.S. achieve above the mean spelling age at 9.

The mean verbal intelligence quotient (Mean of N.F.E.R. PV1 and PV3) was 100.64, S.D. 14.65. The mean family size of the sample was 3.176 children (S.D. 1.693). Of this sample, 8.86% were singletons. The percentage of the sample who

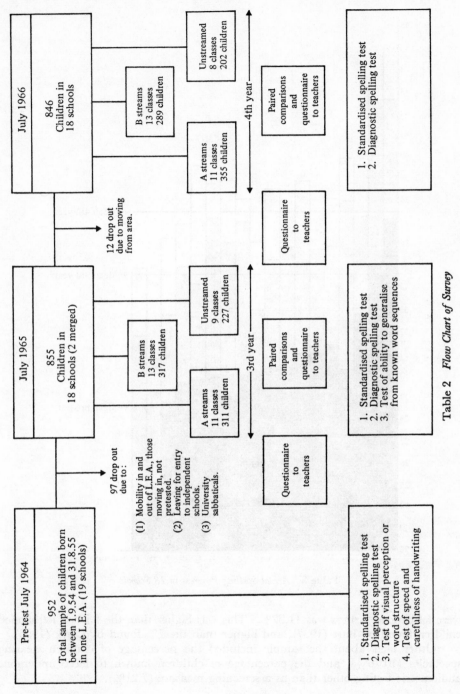

Table 2 *Flow Chart of Survey*

Pre-test July 1964

952
Total sample of children born between 1.9.54 and 31.8.55 in one L.E.A. (19 schools)

1. Standardised spelling test
2. Diagnostic spelling test
3. Test of visual perception or word structure
4. Test of speed and carefulness of handwriting

97 drop out due to:
(1) Mobility in and out of L.E.A., those moving in, not pretested.
(2) Leaving for entry to independent schools.
(3) University sabbaticals.

July 1965

855
Children in 18 schools (2 merged)

A streams
11 classes
311 children

B streams
13 classes
317 children

Unstreamed
9 classes
227 children

3rd year

Questionnaire to teachers

Paired comparisons and questionnaire to teachers

1. Standardised spelling test
2. Diagnostic spelling test
3. Test of ability to generalise from known word sequences

12 drop out due to moving from area.

July 1966

846
Children in 18 schools

A streams
11 classes
355 children

B streams
13 classes
289 children

Unstreamed
8 classes
202 children

4th year

Questionnaire to teachers

Paired comparisons and questionnaire to teachers

1. Standardised spelling test
2. Diagnostic spelling test

23

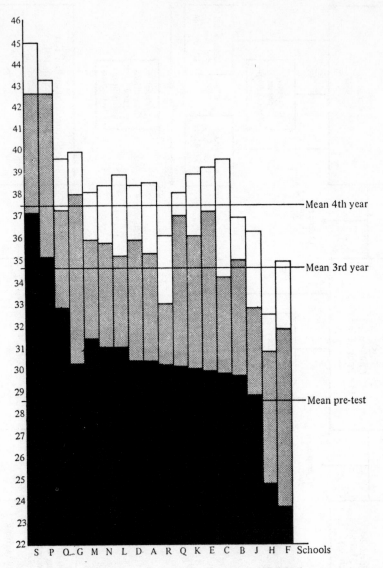

Table 3   *Actual Spelling Progress in 18 Schools*

were lefthanded writers was 11.82%. This was higher than the 5.2% of lefthanded children found by Burt (1937), and higher than the 7% found by Clark (1956).

Other facts about the sample included the percentage of children wearing spectacles (10.76%), and the percentage of children known to have undergone audiometric testing other than as a screening measure (7.21%).

24

In July 1964, the age-group was given a battery of tests by the investigator. The battery consisted of

1. Diagnostic dictation.
2. Test of visual perception of word structure. Test of speed and quality of handwriting.
3. Graded spelling test from the Standard Reading Tests (Daniels and Diack, 1958).

The N.F.E.R. Primary School Verbal Intelligence Test 1 was administered by the school during the same month.

In July 1965, the age-group was given a second battery of tests by the investigator, consisting of

1. Diagnostic dictation.
2. Test of ability to transfer learned word sequences to new words.
3. Graded Spelling Test (Daniels and Diack).

In July 1966 a similar battery was administered including diagnostic dictation and graded spelling test. No supplementary test was given as the children were asked to give certain information, e.g., family place and size, a sufficiently exacting task for many of them. The N.F.E.R. PV3 was administered by the schools.

The Construction of these Tests: tests for second year junior (Table 4) children.

1. Diagnostic dictation of 100 words, was given to standardize what, in an output of free writing, would have been varied in amount and substance. A story that could well have been told by 8–9 year old children was written, containing examples of the commonest types of error, beginning with words the children would be confident that they could spell correctly. 'One day as I was . . .'

In this dictation, 75% of the words occurred in Burrough's first 500 words in his study of the vocabulary of 5–6½ year old children 96% of the words were in his whole list. 4% were not included. These were: Searched, certainly, shaggy and satisfaction. Compared with the N.Z.C.E.R. Alphabetical Spelling List (used at all three levels as a frequency check) 95% of the words occurred in the frequency levels (2,700 words) 5% were outside. These were: Trotting, shaggy, removed, satisfaction, galloped.

All words were compared for difficulty with words in standardized spelling tests. 86% were comparable in difficulty with words spelt correctly by children with a spelling age of 8+.

8% with a spelling age of 9+.
4% with a spelling age of 10+.
2% with a spelling age of 11+ (galloped and satisfaction).

As many phonic combinations, regular and irregular as possible were introduced, 93% conforming to rule. This gave opportunity for children to use their knowledge of rules or spelling precedent also to see where children offer reasonable

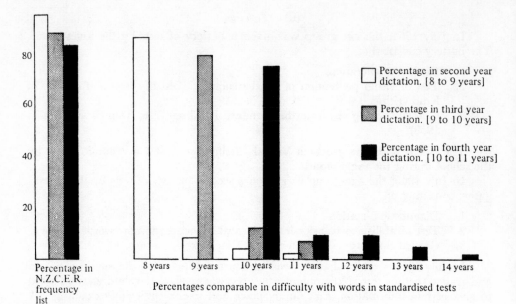

Percentage in second year dictation. [8 to 9 years]

Percentage in third year dictation. [9 to 10 years]

Percentage in fourth year dictation. [10 to 11 years]

Percentage in N.Z.C.E.R. frequency list

Percentages comparable in difficulty with words in standardised tests

Table 4 *Words Occurring in Diagnostic Dictations*

phonic alternatives or where they produce phonic alternatives not conforming to rule. There were 7% grapho-phonemically irregular[1] words, should, said, one, heard, searched, give and where.

2. Two words connected semantically with the dictation were presented on flash cards for specific periods of time in very rigorously controlled conditions. The children looked, and wrote from memory. Exact timing and two supervisors ensured no deviation from instructions. The first word 'Flagrancy' presented for 4 seconds, contained a common regular phonic syllable (flag) and an uncommon but regular phonic syllable 'ancy'. This was aimed at revealing children's ability to reproduce a semantically and visually unfamiliar word from a 4 second exposure. The second word a three syllable regular word 'Vagabond', was exposed for 3 seconds and the children were allowed 10 seconds to write this. This was presented again to reveal the children's ability to reproduce a fairly unfamiliar but regular word, and to reveal their speed and quality of writing. The number of letters achieved, whether right or wrong, and a qualitative judgment of the writing was to be recorded.

3. The Graded Spelling Test from the Standard Reading Tests by Daniels and Diack was presented in its original form.

---

[1] As the result of lively criticism from and discussion with the linguists, the writer is using this far from satisfactory word. It used to be acceptable to say 'phonetically regular', but there is now, as was pointed out in Chapter Two, no completely acceptable alternative.

26

Tests for third year junior children

The second diagnostic dictation for children of 9–10 years again began with familiar words, 'Late one night . . .' In this dictation 88% of the words occurred in the N.Z.C.E.R. frequency levels (2,700 words). 12% were outside this list: Trial-run, helicopter, scarcely, scrambled, glowed, dodged, skilfully, avoid, relief, space-craft, regained and actually. All words were compared for difficulty with words in standardized spelling tests. 79% were comparable in difficulty with words spelt correctly by children with a spelling age of 9+ or under

12%	.....	.....	.....	.....	10+.
7%	.....	.....	.....	.....	11+.
2%	.....	.....	.....	.....	12+.

Again as many phonic combinations, regular and irregular, as possible were introduced, 91% conforming to rule. There were 9% grapho-phonemically irregular words: Friend, would, caught, height, type, one, suit, were, have.

Test 2

To explore the visual learning of coding systems on the basis of learned contingent probabilities, three words were selected from the diagnostic dictation, *suit*, *relief* and *edge*. Different words containing the same coding elements were each exposed for three seconds and written from memory, *fruit*, *field* and *lodge*. This was followed by the writing at oral presentation of three new and unseen words containing the same coding elements and nearer to the original than the visually exposed words, *suitable*, *belief* and *dredge*.

Test 3

The Graded Spelling Test for the Standard Reading Tests of Daniels and Diack was presented. The ceiling of this was not high enough for many of the children, so after consultation with one of the authors (Daniels) of the Graded Spelling Tests, this was amended with words from Schonell's Graded Word Spelling Test A and B. As Schonell's test is scored one word per month of spelling age, and the ceiling of the Daniels and Diack test is 12.3 years, only seven words were added for the 13th year, but 10 each for the 14th and 15th years.

July 1966   Tests for fourth year junior children

Test 1

In the third diagnostic dictation for children of 10–11 years, 83% of the words occurred in the N.Z.C.E.R. frequency levels (2,700 words). 17% were outside this list: Peculiar, approaching, gradually, distinguished, recently, designed, precision, scraping, altimeter, gauge, altitude, alpine, requesting, repairs, enthusiasm, unforgettable, departure. All words were compared for difficulty with words in standardized spelling tests.

75% were comparable in difficulty with words spelled correctly by children with a spelling age of 1C + or under

9% .... 11+.
9% .... 12+.
5% .... 13+.
2% .... 14+.

Again as many phonic combinations, regular and irregular as possible were introduced, 90% conforming to rule or precedent.

There were 10% grapho-phonemically irregular words: Distinguished, designed, aeroplane, machine, gauge, were, anxious, viewed, were, group.

This is the percentage found in a study of words used by children themselves in the course of their writing as collected by Edwards and Gibbon (1963).

Test 2

The Graded Spelling Test (Daniels and Diack) was again presented, again extended beyond its ceiling by Schonell's Graded Word Spelling Test in an alternative form to the one used in the third year.

Further Information about Children

Data were recorded concerning the individual children included sex, socio-economic status, the term of the year in which the child's birthday occurred, the place in family (single, eldest, middle or youngest), the size of the family, handedness, the wearing of spectacles, and the undergoing of an audiometric test other than for screening purposes.

It was noted whether each child was in a streamed school or unstreamed class. Also the mean grade of the teachers by whom the child had been taught during the two years was assessed.

In the fourth year the children were given, by their teachers, a grading of creative writing on a five point scale, according to the following criteria:

A. Very vivid and lively writing.
B. Interesting writing.
C. Writes adequately.
D. Writes but writing dull and uninteresting.
E. Does not achieve written expression beyond very factual and simple level.

(iii) Treatment of data

The diagnostic test scripts were analysed using conventional error categories (Spache, 1940 a and b) except in the case of 'substitution' which was broken down into consonant and vowel substitution of letters, substitution with reasonable phonic alternatives and substitution of phonic alternatives not conforming to rule. The criterion for inclusion in the column 'reasonable phonic alternative' was conformity with precedent. These two latter categories were originally included as it seemed possible that here might appear the effect of training in reading. This in fact appeared so clearly (Chapter Five, Page 65) that substitutions were also broken down in the

28

survey, since it was hypothesized that one of the contributory factors to spelling ability was a rule-following approach to words. The Graded spelling tests were scored, and retained as raw scores, providing a measure of gains from year to year and percentage progress throughout the two years.

Test 2   Second year junior children

From the test of visual perception of word structure the children were graded on a 3 point scale, according to the number and accuracy in serial order of letters they could reproduce. From the untimed handwriting test they were graded for quality of handwriting on a three point scale, the criteria being 'well-formed', 'legible' and 'barely legible'. From the timed handwriting test they were graded on a three point scale for speed according to the number of letters (correct or incorrect) they completed.

Test 2   Third year junior children

From the test of ability to generalize, the children were graded on a three point scale according to their ability to include learned letter sequences in unseen words.

(b)   *Discussion of Analysis of Data*

(i) Comparisons within the variables

It should be mentioned here that there is no significant difference between the sexes in spelling attainment at 9 or 11 years.

There is then information available about four main areas in which spelling ability may be rooted.

These are 1   intrinsic characteristics acquired early in life, i.e. in the pre-school years.
   2   abilities of the kind associated with school learning.
   3   the school.
   4   environmental conditions in the home.

Before analysing the data there are comments to be made about these four areas.

Intrinsic characteristics are presumably acquired 1 in early life or 2 in the early school years. These are all related to verbal ability and inevitably correlated with S.E.S. and family size. It is interesting to look at the proportion of children failing in these categories, e.g., the writing of 22.58% children was 'barely legible' at 9 years.†
42.67% showed poor ability in the auditory perception—encoding—motor process. Again at 9 over half—i.e., 51.54%—when faced with an unknown word made no reasonable attempt (i.e. no attempt at an alternative spelling according to spelling precedent). And at 11, over half, i.e., 55% did not transfer known letter sequences to new words. It is worth noting that carefulness scores (quality of handwriting) at 9 and grades of creative writing at 11 are normally distributed.

---

† See p. 174

3 Examining the distribution of children according to the contribution of the school, there is a slightly skewed distribution of children according to teacher's grade.

15% children are taught by an A teacher*
22%   ,,   ,,   ,,   ,,   B   ,,
27%   ,,   ,,   ,,   ,,   C   ,,
28%   ,,   ,,   ,,   ,,   D   ,,
 8%   ,,   ,,   ,,   ,,   E   ,,

4 In the area of home influence the S.E.S. rating is, by definition, normally distributed.

A correlation matrix of all the variables in these four areas (Table 5) clearly reveals a complex of high inter-correlations around the acquired characteristics of children, and these are associated with spelling attainment at 9 and 11 years. They are highly correlated with socio-economic status and with family size.

It is shown (page 44) in examination of the teacher variable that the teacher's grade of technical skill, which incorporates his rational approach, the manner in which he teaches, marks, exacts corrections and tests, bears a very strong relationship to children's progress. It would be expected then that teachers' grade is influential in the progress of individual children.

There is also a positive correlation between streaming and teacher's grade in the fourth year, i.e. there is a tendency for the more rational teachers to be in the larger streamed schools. This relationship is confirmed in the analysis of the teacher variable when the correlation between teacher's grade and streaming is positive and significant.

(ii) *Regression Analysis*

In order to assess the relative strengths of variables affecting progress in spelling, a series of stepwise regression analyses was performed with actual attainment at 9 and at 11, actual progress from 9 to 10, 10 to 11 and 9 to 11 years, and percentage progress, as dependent variables in turn.

The single most powerful predictor of actual attainment at 9 and at 11 is verbal intelligence. After this, visual perception of word form as tested by the written form is the next most relevant predictor. A somewhat weaker predictor is carefulness as shown in the quality of the child's handwriting. These predictors seem to refer to personal abilities and dispositions acquired by the child in the pre-school years. At 9 years, these characteristics being equal, abilities which are more probably acquired in school can be seen. These are speed of handwriting and fluency (included here, though not assessed until fourth year). A rule-following approach to words and generalization of letter sequences appear to have some very small predictive value at 9 and at 11. Apart from these abilities, home environment (S.E.S., family order and size) can be mentioned at 9, and teacher's grade at 11. However, these are only slightly indicative. A further examination of combinations of predictive variables is considered in the next sub-section.

---

* The grade referring to 'technical skill'.

	1	2	3	4	5	6	7	8	9	10	11	12	13	14	15	16	17
1													HOME			SCHOOL	
2	·88																
3	·74	·77															
4	·69	·68	·62														
5	·61	·57	·50	·54													
6	·57	·53	·47	·43	·43												
7	·69	·72	·70	·58	·47	·46											
8	·63	·61	·58	·60	·44	·40	·54										
9	·63	·67	·60	·61	·44	·40	·53	·55									
10	·65	·63	·63	·61	·47	·43	·60	·55	·54								
11	·46	·57	·69	·47	·33	·33	·58	·45	·53	·46							
12	·41	·43	·49	·30	·26	·22	·45	·31	·29	·32	·46						
13																	
14	·22	·20	·20		·14	·15	·21	·22	·20	·22	·20		·56				
15																	
16																	
17																·22	
18	·32	·21									·22				·19		
19	·22	·19															
20	−·58	−·33	−·30	−·29	−·32	−·27	−·28		−·21	−·26							
21																	
22																	
23																	
24																	

Table 5 *Correlation Matrix   Child Variable*

(All correlations quoted are significant ($p = <0.001$). Blank spaces indicate correlations that are less significant.)

N.B. In the investigation into the teacher variable, the correlation between mean percentage progress of the class and teacher's grade was .45 and between mean actual progress of the class and teacher's grade was .43.

Key:

1	Spelling attainment at 9 years		13	*Home* Place in family
2	Spelling attainment at 11 years		14	*Home* Size of family
3	Verbal intelligence		15	*School* Teacher's grade 9–10
4	Visual perception of word form		16	*School* Teacher's grade 10–11
5	Speed of handwriting		17	*School* Streaming
6	Quality of handwriting		18	Spelling progress 9–10 years
7	Fluency		19	Spelling progress 10–11 years
8	Rule-following approach		20	% progress
9	Generalization		21	Period of year born
10	Auditory perception		22	Handedness
11	11+ selection		23	Vision
12	*Home* S.E.S.		24	Hearing

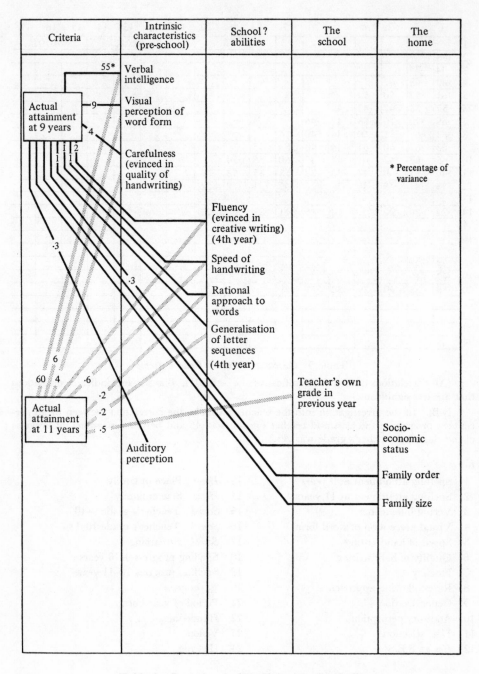

Table 6   *Regression Analysis of Attainment in Spelling*

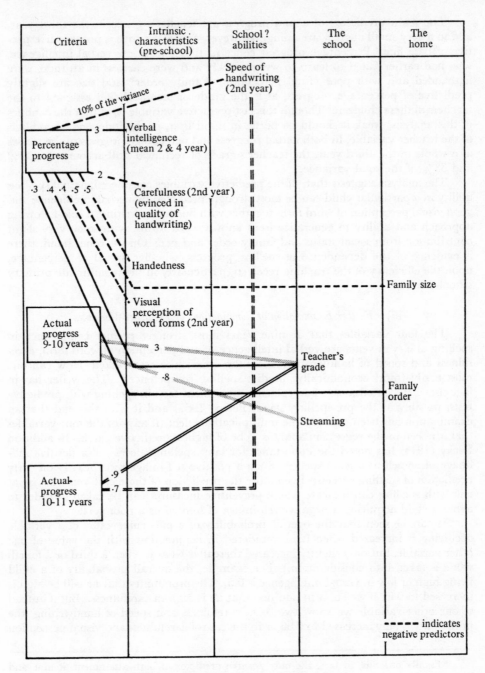

Table 7   *Regression Analysis of Spelling Progress*

The main predictors of actual progress are teacher's grade in the third year, and to a very small degree, streaming. However, actual progress is progress irrespective of base line. Percentage progress concerns those, with low verbal intelligence, who had earlier failed to learn to write quickly and were careless in attitude, were lefthanded and with poor visual perception. Family order* and size are slightly predictive of percentage progress, as is the grade of technical skill assigned to the teachers of these children. Though this last predictive variable is, within the confines of this analysis, weak it should be borne in mind that, in the independent analysis of the teacher variable, in both actual progress and percentage progress of the classes as a whole in the third year, the teacher's grade of technical skill accounts for 30% and 33% of the total variance.

The analysis suggests that, of the predictive variables considered, actual spelling ability in a particular child can be most strongly predicted by verbal intelligence and good visual perception of word form together with fluency in writing, a rule-following approach and ability to generalize from known word forms, with some very slight contribution from social status and family order and size. On the other hand, there is evidence of the dependence of spelling progress, whether actual or percentage, upon the efficiency of the teaching received, particularly in the penultimate primary school year.

(iii)   *Further Examination of Combinations of Predictive Variables*

The four variables that at nine years most strongly predict competence in spelling at eleven years are verbal intelligence, visual perception of word form, carefulness and speed of handwriting. Now the question is often asked 'How can one most easily (most economically) predict spelling competence?' The writer has in fact elsewhere stated a case for replacing attainment tests in spelling with predictive tests, possibly at the pre-spelling stage (Peters, 1967) and it is to this end that an examination has been made of the multiplicative effect (if any) of the four variables that are seen in the regression analysis to be of highest predictive value. In addition Lecky (1945) has noted the importance for later spelling success, of a positive self-image of oneself as a good speller. Such a positive self-image rests heavily on early prediction of spelling success. Even more the prediction of those children who are at risk with spelling can indicate where preventive measures can be taken in order to avoid a child acquiring a negative self-image of himself as a poor speller.

It can be seen that the overall probability of a particular value of a variable occurring is increased when it is considered in conjunction with the value of one other variable, but only slightly increased thereafter (that is when a third or a fourth value is taken into consideration.) For example, the overall probability of a child being high or low in verbal intelligence is 0.5. The probability that he will be high is increased to 0.83 if we know in addition that he is high in carefulness. But if instead of one other variable we know two; e.g., carefulness and speed of handwriting, the probability is only increased to 0.86 or in the case of carefulness and visual perception

---

* Family order is, in fact, the only positive predictor of both attainment at nine and percentage progress.

34

of word form to 0.9. Yet if all *three* variables are high in addition to verbal intelligence, the revised probability is only .89. In other words, knowledge of one extra variable is proportionately much more useful than knowledge of two or three extras (subject to the law of diminishing returns). Of course the nature of the added variable affects the probability estimate, but it is fairly clear that two good predictors should be enough and that further predictors may even cloud the issue.

The question then is what is the minimal amount of information about a particular child that will fairly certainly predict competence or incompetence in spelling? It would seem that two strong predictors would be almost as useful as three or four, and the question is then, which? Mean scores of those children's spelling attainment at eleven years who obtained combinations of high, medium and low scores in the four variables at nine years were calculated. (Appendix D). Categories were excluded in which there were fewer than ten children (i.e., less than 1% of the sample) obtaining the particular combination (e.g., only eight children in the whole sample were high in speed, carefulness and visual perception of word form, but low in verbal intelligence). There were eighteen categories remaining, and these were plotted in relation to the upper or lower halves of mean attainment in spelling at eleven years (Table 8). Comparison was made between categories where two variables were both high, and where they were *not* both high, and categories where both variables were

Table 8 *Categories of combinations of predictive variables at 9 years in relation to upper and lower halves of mean attainment in spelling at 11 years*

	V_1 and V_2		V_1 and V_3		V_1 and V_4		V_2 and V_3		V_2 and V_4		V_3 and V_4	
	UH	LH	UH	LH	UH	LH	UH	LH	UH	LH	UH	LH
Both high	2	—	5	—	3		2		1		2	
Not both high	7	9	4	9	6	9	7	9	8	9	7	9
Both low	—	1	—	2	—	2	—	6	2	4	—	6
Not both low	9	8	9	7	9	7	9	3	7	5	9	3

V_1 = Speed of handwriting. (Grades 1, 2, 3.)
V_2 = Carefulness (Grades 1, 2, 3.)
V_3 = Verbal intelligence. (Grades 0 and 1. 1 = above median 101; 0 = below median 101.)
V_4 = Visual perception of word form. (Grades 1, 2, 3.)

Numbers of children in whom combinations of predictive variables occur at 9 years, and their attainment in spelling (upper and lower halves of combination means at 11 years)

	V_1 and V_2		V_1 and V_3		V_1 and V_4		V_2 and V_3		V_2 and V_4		V_3 and V_4	
	UH	LH	UH	LH	UH	LH	UH	LH	UH	LH	UH	LH
Both high	90	—	328	11	244	10	90	11	66	—	219	—
Not both high	285	375	47	305	131	365	285	364	309	375	166	365
Both low	—	1	—	59	—	59	—	194	—	163	—	220
Not both low	375	374	375	316	375	316	375	181	375	212	375	145

low and where they were *not* both low. It can be seen that of the four variables that seem to be of high predictive value, if speed and verbal intelligence are both high there is a 0.55 probability that the children will be in the upper half of spelling attainment at eleven. It can also be seen that if either carefulness *or* visual perception of word form is low together with low verbal intelligence, there is a 0.67 probability that the children will be in the lower half of spelling attainment at eleven years. (If instead of categories, the number of children in each category is examined, the probability increases in the case of writing and verbal intelligence both being high, to 0.9, but in the case of two variables being low, the probability slightly decreases. This is because of the large number (20% of the sample) of children in the 1, 2, 1, 1 category, i.e., high in everything except carefulness (which is rated medium). This raises the probability level of the predictors in the upper half of spelling attainment but does not significantly affect those in the lower half).

It is not surprising that lack of care is, with poor verbal intelligence, a predictor of poor spelling ability. Holmes (1959) while showing that only a small area of spelling success or failure could be attributed to personality factors, nevertheless indicated a relationship between poor spelling and a casual attitude generally.

With a child of high verbal intelligence, then, there is a good chance that he will be a good speller at eleven if he is also a quick writer, but with a child of low verbal intelligence the chances are weighted against his being good at spelling if, in addition, he is not a careful child or if his visual perception of word form is weak. In fact if any two of the three conditions, poor verbal intelligence, poor visual perception of word form and lack of care are present, this child is at risk as far as spelling goes.

It is clear that it is easier to predict poor spelling than good spelling, and that there are more combinations of predictors of poor spelling. This sub-section indicates the need for future work in the area of prediction of spelling failure, rather than in the field of testing.

(c) *Summary of Results*

The overall picture obtained from examining the data related to the child variable reveals a complex of inter-correlations around acquired characteristics associated with spelling attainment, and of these *verbal intelligence* is the most powerful predictor, followed by *visual perception of word forms*, and then *carefulness* evinced in quality of handwriting. Other acquired abilities that are slightly predictive are *speed of writing* and a *rational approach to words*. At 9 years, *socio-economic status*, and at 11 years, *teacher's own grade* of technical skill in the previous year are slightly predictive.

In the case of percentage progress, we are dealing with less favoured children, those, in fact whose abilities, particularly *speed of handwriting* are very poor. Here the positive influence on progress is *teacher's own grade* and family order. This is interesting since it indicates that the less favoured child *can* progress if well taught, and that these children progress even though starting with many disadvantages, if they have the advantage of being in a favourable family position, viz: singleton or eldest rather than youngest or middle.

36

From examination of combinations of predictive variables it is seen to be easier to predict poor spelling than good spelling. It would seem that if a child is high in verbal intelligence and also able to write swiftly the spelling prognosis is good, but that if a child scores low in any two out of the three predictors, verbal intelligence, visual perception of word form and carefulness, he is at risk in the field of spelling competence.

(d)   *Examination of Evidence Concerning Generalizing Ability*

The results of the investigation so far indicate where we stand in the incidental/ systematic controversy. Favoured children acquire the ability. Less-favoured children can acquire the ability by good teaching especially when, to some extent, family-supported.

But there is one basic aspect of spelling ability, however, that relates, as was shown in Section Two, to generalizing of letter sequences. To supplement investigation of the child variable, careful examination of this generalizing ability was essential.

It was appropriate, then, to examine two intercorrelated variables (both of which appear as predictors in the major analyses of attainment, though not of progress) that are specifically concerned with word structure, viz.: rule-following approach, and generalization of letter sequence. These were tested in different ways and at different times, but tapped the same ability since in both cases spelling precedent was the criterion. This generalizing ability is acquired by those of high verbal intelligence. It is not something that can be picked up by the less verbally intelligent unless they are very sensitive to word form. It must, in fact, be learned by attending to the teacher's deliberate pointing out of word structure via rational, systematic, time-consuming methods.

This is not always thought to be the case. In addition to teachers' hopeful expectation that good spelling will be 'caught' by the less competent speller as he reads more, there is occasionally voiced an assumption that children will, 'in the process of maturation', acquire spelling ability. Now competence in spelling, it has been argued, entails the ability to generalize from serial probability, and this generalizing ability is expected by some teachers to emerge Piaget-wise, independently of experience. But this generalizing capacity is not a logical operation (competent spelling, as Schonell pointed out, is automatic, predictable, infallible) but merely a strategic element in a skill. And skills are acquired by imitation, by successive approximation, and above all by practice. Opportunities for these are made available by the teacher. And here is exposed the paradox of spelling since this investigation leads us to think that spelling is ultimately not a rational activity, yet one that can best be taught by rational methods.

Design

To test the hypothesis that generalizing ability is acquired by children in the process of maturation, and to examine the effect of minimal participation in the learning of this skill, the range of schools was examined to see where, if at all, there had been no teaching of spelling in the third year of the junior school.

The third year (children aged nine to ten years) was the year of greatest interest since this is the year in which the greatest improvement in spelling, throughout the sample, occurs. In addition there was information as to the extent to which a child was able to generalize from known word sequences at the end of the second year and at the end of the third year.

There were only two classes in which, throughout the third year (and indeed in one of these, Class O, throughout the two years) there was no list learning, no instruction and no testing. To examine whether, by 'maturation', children acquired the ability to generalize from known word sequences (irrespective of teaching), spelling attainment, percentage progress, and the extent of improvement and deterioration in generalizing ability were examined, with a view to comparing these with the whole age group.

One of the two, Class R, was a slightly streamed class from which the least able children had been transferred to another class, and hence the initial spelling attainment was slightly but not significantly higher than in the age group as a whole. In this class there was a minimal time of fifty minutes per week spent in creative writing (whole population mean: 139 minutes, S.D.: 64.9) with no exacting of corrections. The teacher of this class commented, 'The supposed rules of English spelling elude me and I do not propose to inflict them on the class', and 'Occasionally spelling bees give the more able a chance to reveal their virtuosity'. In this class, actual progress and percentage progress were significantly lower than in the age-group as a whole. No child improved in generalizing ability and 18% of the children actually deteriorated during the year. But this was an unusual class in that the teacher was actively opposed to spelling, and gave little time or encouragement to creative writing.

It was decided then to look more carefully at School O, where, though no teaching of spelling of any kind occurred, considerable time was given to creative writing (220 minutes per week). Corrections were exacted, though at a rote not rational level. The teacher commented, 'About ten minutes daily, used for follow-up to written work, writing words four times and entering in word books. If the words are going to "stick" I feel this is sufficient.' Class O, slightly but not significantly higher in socio-economic status, was also slightly but not significantly higher in initial attainment than the age-group as a whole, and hence in rational attack. It was completely unstreamed. This provided a climate more comparable with the population as a whole, for examining the hypothesis that generalizing ability could be acquired without teaching.

Individual children in the third year could do one of three things; improve, deteriorate, or maintain their state of being able or not able to generalize. In the 'year' as a whole, 12.18% of the children improved in ability; in School O, only 3% of the children improved. In the year as a whole 11.35% deteriorated in this ability; in School O, loss of ability to generalize occurred in 24%. In other words, 24% children who were able to generalize at nine, were no longer able to do so at ten, while 3%, unable to generalize at nine, had learned to do so at ten. Thus in comparison with the age-group as a whole, School O deteriorated in generalizing ability significantly (p = <0.01).

This is despite the fact that, looking at means, actual spelling progress in the third year in School O (Mean 4.41; S.D. 3.6) reflects the actual progress in the whole of the age group (Mean 5.45; S.D. 4.33). This conformity is repeated in the fourth year. (School O: Mean 2.67; S.D. 7.9; Whole age group Mean 2.65; S.D. 3.40). As would be expected the mean percentage progress is less (p = <0.01) in School O than in the whole age-group. Hence, far from arriving at the ability to generalize being untaught, of the children in this school, whose rule-following approach deteriorated in the first of these two years (i.e., the third year junior, nine to ten years) all except one were still making significantly more unreasonable than reasonable attempts at words they did not know. Only one, by the age of eleven, had re-established his technique of using spelling precedent as a guide when confronted with words he did not know, e.g., de*sigh*ned, pre*si*tion, whereas at ten he had offered *squlluly* for skilfully, and *caghthacefrell* for comfortable.

Table 9 *The Effect of No Spelling Teaching on the Ability to Generalize*

| | | School O | | Whole Sample | | |
		Mean	S.D.	Mean	S.D.	
Actual Progress	3rd yr.	4.41	3.6	5.45	4.33	n.s.
	4th yr.	2.67	7.9	2.65	3.40	n.s.
% Progress		14.57%	12.24	19.73%	8.66	p = <0.01
Improvement		3%		12.18%		p = <0.01
Deterioration		24%		11.35%		p = <0.01

Discussion of Findings

It would seem that competence in spelling necessitates a qualitative change in spelling behaviour for most children in the junior school. This change entails children learning to make a reasonable attempt in accordance with sequential probability, i.e., in accordance with spelling precedent. This ability to generalize may coincide with the development of formal operational thinking, but it is clear from the evidence in the case of this particular skill that such generalization is dependent on rational and systematic teaching procedures.

IV Teaching Variable

(a) *Design*

(i) *Subjects*

The 952 children were in 32 classes in the third year, and 33 classes in the fourth year, involving 58 teachers. Six of these teachers retained the class throughout the two years, but as their attitude and their behaviour varied according to the 'year' they were teaching, these were included in both third and fourth year analyses. Three teachers appear twice in this sample but with different classes. Thus, although there were only 56 teachers, the number in the sample is 65. Of the sample of individual teachers there was an equal number of men and women (28). Throughout the investigation there was only one refusal by a teacher, and this was of a confirmatory questionnaire, in which the information had already been acquired in another way.

It was never made explicit that the investigator was studying spelling and the paired comparisons questionnaire concerning attitudes to creative writing seemed to cloud for the teachers the aim of the exercise at any rate in the early stages of the investigation.

(ii) *Techniques*

During the Spring Term of 1965 and again of 1966 the appended questionnaire (P. 86) was given to the teachers of this age-group. The times of each of the aspects of teaching behaviour concerned with spelling were completed and compared.

During the Summer Term teachers were asked to make Paired Comparisons and complete a second questionnaire (P. 87). The paired comparisons were analysed and a coefficient of consistence (k) was obtained for each teacher. The replies were corroborated in interview with the teacher.

The following Spring 1966 the questionnaire (P. 86) was again given to the teachers of the age-group. This was similar, except that the following question was added: 'Have you, in the past year, had much discussion of spelling, formal or informal in your school?' By this time it was probable that the teachers were aware of what was being investigated and answers to this question were likely to indicate any unprecedented and excessive attention to the skill.

(iii) *Treatment of Data*

This section of the investigation measured and analysed the teaching behaviour and attitudes of the 65 teachers who taught these 846 children and the relationships between these teacher variables and progress in spelling.

More specifically, the enquiry dealt with five main teacher variables and sub-variables itemized below. Measures on each variable were obtained for each teacher and inter-correlated. These individual teacher measures were also correlated with the mean percentage progress of the teacher's class during the year.

1. Attitudes of teachers to what is important in children's free-writing. (Table 10).

2. Teachers' grades of technical skill according to the following indices: consistency of policy, no matter in what direction; regular and systematic testing; active and rational marking practice on the part of the teacher and correction practice on the part of the child. (Table 11).

3. How teachers teach spelling:
    (*a*) Whether lists of spelling are or are not taught
    (*b*) If taught, the kinds of lists used
        (i) Printed lists., e.g., Schonell
        (ii) Words asked for in the course of the children's free writing
        (iii) Teacher prepared lists
    (*c*) The time spent on list learning and on spelling instruction
    (*d*) The total time spent on spelling
    (*e*) The total time spent on creative writing
    (*f*) 'Corrections' practice
    (*g*) The 'trying out' of words

4. Testing Practice
    (*a*) The time spent on testing
    (*b*) The frequency of testing
        (i) not at all
        (ii) irregularly
        (iii) daily
        (iv) weekly
    (*c*) The organization of testing
        (i) not at all
        (ii) individually
        (iii) as a group
        (iv) as a class

5. The mean socio-economic status of the children in each class assessed on father's occupation considered in relation to progress in spelling and to each of the above variables.

(b) *Discussion of Analysis of Data*

(i) *Comparisons within the variables*

The data concerning the attitudes and behaviour of the 65 teachers in the sample was analysed in various ways. Initially the data was examined in detail, comparisons being made within the variables. Next a correlation matrix was produced (Table 19). This provided the basis for a factorial analysis from which particular patterns of teacher behaviour emerged. Finally a regression analysis was performed with mean actual progress and mean percentage progress as dependent variables in turn.

These different forms of analysis revealed different areas of interest in teacher behaviour. They will be discussed in turn.

D

1. Attitudes of Teachers to Free-Writing

Table 10 *Attitudes Revealed by Paired Comparisons made by 65 Teachers*

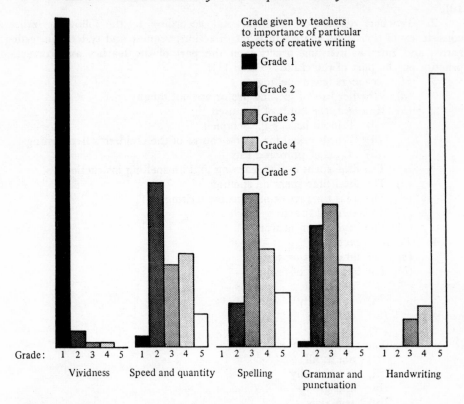

Grade given by teachers
to importance of particular
aspects of creative writing

■ Grade 1
■ Grade 2
■ Grade 3
□ Grade 4
□ Grade 5

Grade: 1 2 3 4 5   1 2 3 4 5   1 2 3 4 5   1 2 3 4 5   1 2 3 4 5

Vividness   Speed and quantity   Spelling   Grammar and punctuation   Handwriting

The attitudes of the teachers of the 65 classes in the age-group to the importance of various aspects of children's free-writing were ascertained by paired comparisons in the course of acquiring a measure of the consistency of individual teachers.

Attitudes of the teachers of the 65 classes in the age-group to the importance of various aspects of children's free-writing elicited by the method of paired comparisons

Aspects of Children's Writing	Importance attributed by teachers				
	A	B	C	D	E
Vividness of writing	92.3%	4.6%	1.5%	1.5%	0
Speed and quantity of output	3.1%	46.1%	23.1%	26.1%	9.2%
Spelling	0	12.3%	43.07%	27.7%	15.3%
Grammar and punctuation	1.5%	33.8%	4.0%	23.1%	0

The emphasis on vividness, followed by speed and quantity of output and the rejection of handwriting as being important was to be expected. There is uncertainty

42

overall about the importance of grammar and punctuation. A third of the teachers place it second, and nearly a quarter fourth. Spelling is in a much more predictable position. 43% put it in middle place, which suggests that this is an ability to be considered but not emphasized.

Table 11 *Teacher's Grades of Technical Skill Related to Mean Percentage Progress of Their Classes*

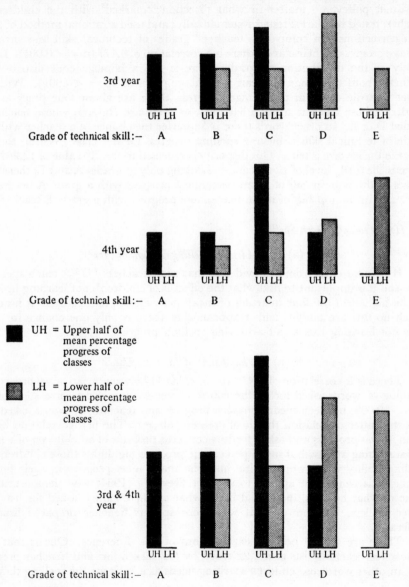

The consistency coefficient (Kendall) was not found to correlate significantly with any other of the teachers' attributes or practices but it was one of the indices contributing to the teacher's grade of technical skill.

2. Teachers' Grades of Technical Skill

This was assigned to the teacher on the basis of whether she had or had not a consistent policy, no matter in what direction; 'marked' with the children (i.e., taught); tested regularly; tested systematically; and used a rational method of dealing with corrections. In comparing teachers' grades of technical skill and mean percentage progress in their classes, there is a correlation of 0.477 (p = <0.001). Looking closely at the distribution of grades there is not a homogeneous distribution of teachers about the range of mean percentage progress (p = <0.001). Within the upper quartile of mean percentage progress, there are about four times as many children whose teachers are graded A–C, as there are children whose teachers are graded D or E. In other words there is a quarter the chance of a teacher with a low grade of technical skill achieving spelling progress for her class. Within the lower quartile the reverse is true. This disparity is reflected in the X^2 value of 12.262 which exceeds the 0.1% level of significance. Looking only at grades A and E, there are no classes in the bottom *half* of mean percentage progress with a grade A teacher, and no classes in the top *half* of mean percentage progress with a grade E teacher.

3. How Teachers Teach Spelling

(a) Are Lists of Spelling Taught or Not?

It is quite clear from the evidence that most teachers (77%) teach spelling by lists, and it is important to find what the effect is of children's not learning lists at all. In the highest of the four quartiles of mean percentage progress there is no class in which no lists are taught, and it appears that there is only one chance in six of a class not learning lists at all achieving spelling progress.

(b) What Kinds of Lists are Used?

There is a correlation of 0.412 (p = <0.001) between mean *actual* progress and teaching of 'words asked for' in the course of free-writing and a correlation of 0.338 (p = <0.006) between mean *percentage* progress and teaching of 'words asked for'— It is this latter correlation that is of greatest interest. The first correlation between mean actual progress and asked for lists concerns progress of all children of whatever initial spelling ability, but mean percentage progress highlights those children whose spelling ability was lowest at nine but who made most progress in their final two years. This would not appear to support Freyberg (1964) who demonstrated the value of what he calls 'individual lists' (what are here called 'asked for lists') with better spellers, but showed that with poor spellers 'teacher prepared lists' were preferable.

There are several possible explanations of this difference. One is that of the 51 teachers teaching lists at all, 22 teach by *both* 'asked for' and 'teacher prepared'. lists, in other words use children's writing needs as a basis for the spelling they teach

Indeed it is difficult for a thoughtful and rational teacher to separate the two, since the words 'asked for' often spark off possible alternatives for the teacher and child who are alive to the possibilities of vocabulary and linguistic extension.

Table 12   *Source of Words Learned*

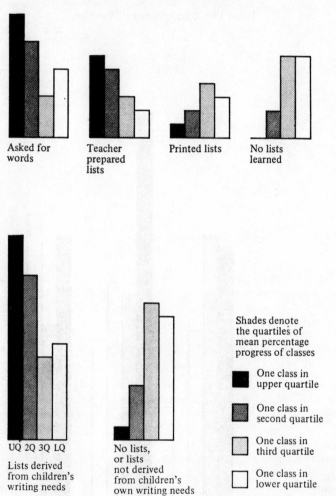

A much more realistic contrast is between the progress of classes where lists learned derive from childrens' writing needs, either direct (asked for words) or indirect (teacher prepared lists) as opposed to learning from printed lists or no list learning at all. There is here a significant difference (p = <0.001) between the mean percentage progress and these two approaches.

(c) *How much Time is spent on List Learning and on Spelling Instruction?*

The difference here is not merely between learning and teaching. The difference clearly reflects the individual bias of teachers, e.g., one teacher who did no list learning and no testing spent ten minutes a day on 'instruction' but this was largely related to marking and the exacting of 'corrections'. Another teacher's class spent

Table 13 *Actual Progress: Time Spent*

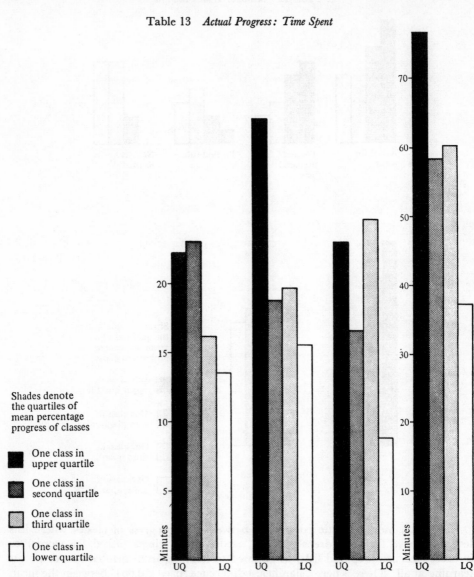

Shades denote
the quartiles of
mean percentage
progress of classes

One class in
upper quartile

One class in
second quartile

One class in
third quartile

One class in
lower quartile

46

ten minutes a day on list learning and fifteen minutes each Friday on the words learned being tested. This particular teacher also pursued a less rational marking and correction policy. This is not to say that list learning and less rational marking and correction behaviour are incompatible. There is, in fact, a significant negative correlation (−0.34) between a rational corrections policy and the learning of printed lists.* This fact is discussed later in connection with regression analysis. The difference between classes in the upper half and lower half of mean percentage progress in time spent on list learning is significant (p = <0.025). The difference in time spent in instruction is only significant (p = <.05) between the top and bottom quartiles of mean percentage progress and the trend is by no means as consistent as with time spent on list learning.

Table 14   *Percentage Progress: Time Spent*

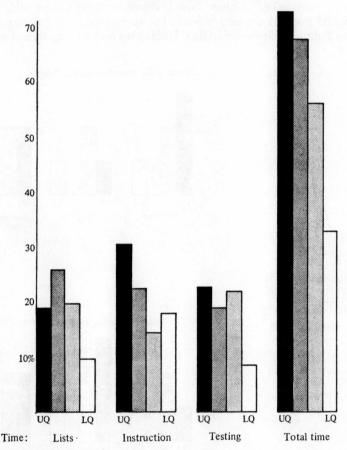

---

* Factor *3* in Factor Analysis 2, Page 56.

(d) *Is the Total Time spent on Spelling Significant?*

As would be expected, total time spent on spelling was correlated (0.486) with mean percentage progress.

(e) *Does the Time spent on Creative Writing in School affect Spelling Progress?*

It was originally hypothesized that time spent on creative writing would correlate with progress in spelling. In fact this is shown to be non-significant. Now time spent on creative writing correlates significantly (0.38) with 'asked for' list learning, but not with any of the variables related to rationality of marking, correction policy, testing procedures, or teachers' grade of technical skill.

(f) *Corrections Practice: Rational or Rote?*

Teachers were asked to show how children in their classes 'did' corrections. Answers varied from 'Write each mistake out three times'—to techniques involving the children finding their own mistakes, looking up and writing them from memory.

Table 15 *Percentage Pursuing Rational Corrections Policy*

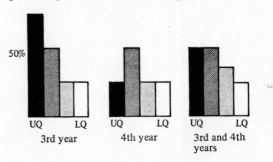

Shades denote
the quartiles of
mean percentage
progress of classes

■ One class in
upper quartile

▨ One class in
second quartile

▢ One class in
third quartile

▢ One class in
lower quartile

Percentage Pursuing Rote Corrections Policy

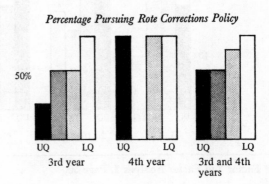

48

It is possible to separate such 'rote' from 'rational' practices, for most rational practices involve some autonomy of learning, active self-testing, etc. The hypothesis was that children who are taught to 'do' corrections in a rational manner make progress in spelling. This correlation between rational correction practice and mean percentage progress was in fact 0.333 (p = <0.007).

The percentage of rational correction technique in the four quartiles was as follows:

	U.Q.	2nd Q.	3rd Q.	L.Q.
IIIrd year	75%	50%	50%	25%
IVth year	25%	50%	25%	25%
IIIrd and IVth year	50%	50%	37.5%	25%

which suggests that the less progress made, the less rational the system of corrections. It is interesting to note that correction is less rational in the fourth than in the third year, the year, in fact, when greatest progress in spelling occurs. The difference between progress in classes subjected to rational as opposed to rote correction technique is significant (p = <0.01).

(g)   Is 'Trying Out' of Words Encouraged?

Teachers were asked if they advised children to 'try' the word before asking or looking it up. The hypothesis was that trying out a word would emphasize uncertainty and reinforce errors, and attention could not be drawn by the teacher to the 'hard spots', as would happen if the spelling was 'asked for'. The correlation between mean percentage progress and 'trying out' of words is 0.253 (p = <0.039), so there is some slight relationship between progress and trying out words.

It may be that the teachers who profess to telling children to 'try out' words do so positively, with the connotation 'Try it out and discover at what point you have difficulty.' It may be that this 'trying out' is to the teacher an indication of positive action. One statement runs 'Children bring me attempts written on pieces of paper provided during written work. Corrected or sent back to look in dictionary according to ability. Children have then to show the word in the dictionary.' Or another: 'phonetic' and syllable principles for thinking it out individually' (an ill expressed but positive statement). Or 'I tell the children to make a good attempt if they do not know the spelling, others to look it up when they had finished the piece of writing.'

This question evidently exposed an attitude to autonomy in the children's learning to spell, rather than the differential effect of trying an unknown word or asking for it to be written. Such a difference could be explored experimentally. Note was taken of mention of the use of the dictionary but the results were non-significant.

4.   How Teachers test Spelling

Testing practice was explored in three ways:

For one particular week, the time spent on testing was recorded. Teachers were asked if they tested spelling daily or weekly, and they were asked if they tested spelling individually, in groups or as a class.

A cluster of correlations (Table 20) depicts the associations between time spent, frequency, organization of testing and mean percentage progress.

(a) *Does Testing in fact Take Place?*

When teachers were asked if testing occurred in their classes it appeared that only one class in the top quartile of classes ranked for mean percentage progress experienced no testing at all, though there were six in the lowest quartile. There is one chance in eight of a class experiencing no testing achieving spelling progress.

(b) *How much Time is spent on Testing?*

As would be expected, there is a significant ($p = <0.001$) correlation (0.365) between the amount of time spent on testing and mean percentage progress.

(c) *What is the Frequency and Organization of such Testing?*

Weekly testing was regular testing and correlated significantly 0.305 ($p = <0.01$) with mean percentage progress. There is a three to one chance of classes receiving regular testing achieving spelling progress.

In the two classes where testing was reported to occur daily, testing was carried out individually, which implies that many children would not be tested on some days. These two classes would be assigned to the haphazard rather than the systematic category, and mean percentage progress is significantly different ($p = <0.01$).

Breaking down the information about testing, it can be seen that though some weekly testing was reported to be in groups by a sixth of the sample and individually by a sixth, two thirds of the classes tested weekly were tested as a class. Indeed 50% of all the classes in the age groups were tested weekly as a class.

Table 16

Summary of Results	
Variable Mean percentage progress	*TEACHING*
Teacher's grade of technical skill	*VARIABLE*
	$p = <0.001$
Use of Lists:	
Lists derived from children's demands in the course of their free writing	$p = <0.006$)
Lists derived from children's demands and teacher prepared lists	$p = <0.001$
Time Spent:	
Time on list learning	$p = <0.025$
Time on instruction	$p = <0.05$
Time on creative writing	n.s.
Correction Technique:	
Rational correction practice	$p = <0.007$
Trying out of words	n.s.
Testing Practice:	
Time spent	$p = <0.001$
Systematic testing	$p = <0.01$

There is a marked association between percentage progress in spelling and weekly class testing. It is three times as likely that a class's spelling will progress if it is tested weekly as a class, than weekly as a group or individually. This is presumably because class testing is systematic. It is four times as likely that a class's spelling will progress if it is tested as a class weekly than if it is tested irregularly.

The following summary relates to mean percentage progress, highlighting the less favoured children. (It is interesting to note that the effect of use of lists derived from children's writing needs is strongest ($p = <0.001$) in the case of mean actual progress).

Table 17   *Breakdown of Information About Regularity and Organization of Testing*

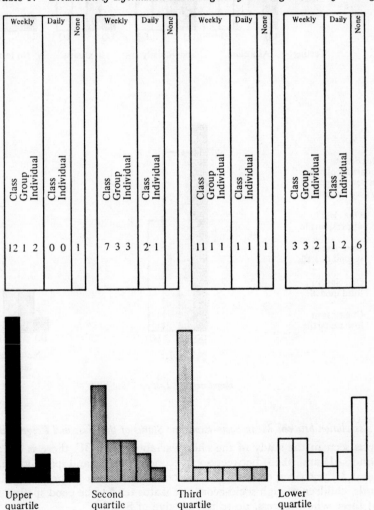

| Upper quartile | Second quartile | Third quartile | Lower quartile |

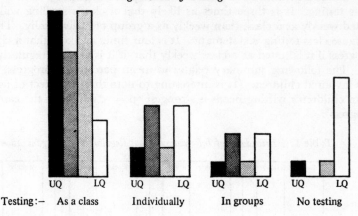

Table 18 *Organization of Testing*

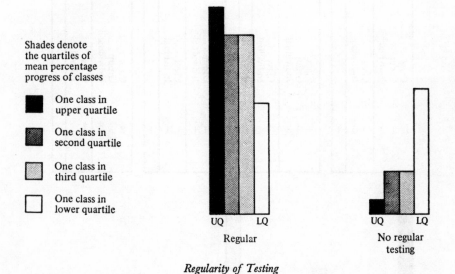

Shades denote
the quartiles of
mean percentage
progress of classes

One class in
upper quartile

One class in
second quartile

One class in
third quartile

One class in
lower quartile

Regularity of Testing

5. *The Association between Mean Socio-Economic Status of the Class and Progress in Spelling*

As was seen in the study of the child variable (Page 31) there is a significant correlation (0.41) and (0.43) between socio-economic status and spelling *attainment* at 9 years and 11 years respectively, but no correlation with *progress* in spelling. In other words, children of high socio-economic status tend to be good spellers from the start, but those who progress, do so irrespective of S.E.S.

52

Looking, however, at school means, the *mean* S.E.S. will reflect the area in which the school is situated and the preponderance of middle or working class children in attendance. Looking at this school variable, certain interesting trends can be observed. The lower the school S.E.S., the higher the percentage progress, since the children in these schools tend to begin at a lower attainment level. The lower the school S.E.S., the greater the total time spent on the teaching of spelling, the more time spent testing spelling, but the less time spent on creative writing.

(ii) *Factor Analysis*

A maximum likelihood and varimax rotation factor analysis (Clarke, 1966) was performed on 23 variables relating to the 65 teachers and their classes. Five factors emerged, but of these the first factor accounted for 16.4% of the total variance, while only 7% variance was accounted for by the second factor. This means that this first factor is more than twice as important as the second or any other of the factors in terms of the percentage variance.

Table 19   *Correlation Matrix   Teaching Variable*

	1	2	3	4	5	6	7	8	9	10	11	12	13	14	15	16
1																
2	·85															
3	−·24	·06														
4	−·18	−·05	·35													
5	·31	·28	−·07	·03												
6	·27	·29	−·12	−·20	·61											
7	·33	·30	−·03	·13	−·05	−·12										
8	·45	·43	−·08	·08	·54	·55	·32									
9	·22	·21	·02	·03	·47	·26	·02	·16								
10	−·18	−·13	−·08	−·22	·29	·23	−·34	·05	·26							
11	·12	·19	−·04	·13	·35	·18	−·01	·12	·08	·04						
12	·34	·41	−·04	·38	·26	·23	·05	·07	·19	·05	·01					
13	·25	·27	−·05	−·14	·18	·16	−·09	·21	·15	·07	−·06	·09				
14	·28	·22	−·16	−·15	·42	·48	·03	·31	·38	·32	·24	·21	·12			
15	·34	·33	−·20	·22	·06	·05	·33	·24	·16	−·16	−·01	−·01	·06	·03		
16	·34	·23	−·29	−·11	·44	·35	·10	·47	·44	·33	·14	·21	·21	·33	·19	
17	·49	·41	−·32	·01	·43	·42	·25	·49	·47	·21	·17	·19	·18	X	X	X

(Above ·24 significant at 5% level)

(Above ·31 significant at 1% level)

(X indicates that this correlation is omitted because the two variables are interdependent)

Key:

1 Mean percentage progress of class
2 Mean actual progress of class
3 Mean S.E.S. of class
4 Time spent on creative writing
5 Regular testing
6 Organized testing
7 Rational corrections practice
8 Teachers' grades
9 Lists of spellings learned
10 Learning: printed lists
11 Learning: teacher prepared lists
12 Learning: asked for lists
13 Practice encouraged of 'trying out' words
14 Time spent on learning lists
15 Time spent on instruction
16 Time spent on testing
17 Total time on spelling

Table 20

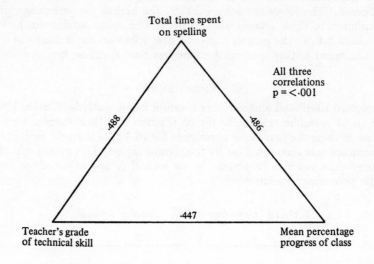

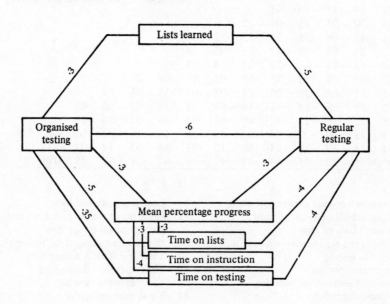

This first factor is obvious if one merely looks at the correlation matrix. It appears as a cluster of correlations, which in its simplest form is shown in Table 20.

This factor is a teacher factor in which the main loadings are as follows (in this order):

> Teacher's grade
> Total time spent on spelling
> Testing practice frequency
> Time spent on testing
> Testing practice organization
> Mean percentage progress
> Time spent on lists
> Rational corrections practice
> Practice of trying out of words
> Teaching by 'asked for' lists

The highest negative loading is the *year* in which a child happens to be; obviously of no matter to a really good teacher who teaches conscientiously wherever she is placed.

The remaining factors are concerned with teachers' attitudes. The second factor deals with whether teachers are concerned with quality or quantity of written work. The third factor is very interesting. It is concerned with whether teachers are consistent in their attitudes, as opposed to pursuing a vague and unorganized 'creative' approach. With a high *consistency* loading is also a high *attitude to spelling* loading as well as a high loading of *time spent on* creative writing and *rational corrections* procedure. At the other pole is a strong *attitude in favour of vividness* loading, which is more likely to occur in *high S.E.S. schools*. So a strong attitude in favour of vividness does not necessarily go with time and trouble spent on creative writing by teachers consistent in their policy.

Having extracted in the analysis how teachers deal with content, the fourth and fifth factors are concerned with attitude to form, i.e., *how* rather than *what* children are taught to write. The fourth factor is concerned with whether teachers think the *appearance* is more important than, at the other pole, *spelling*, and the fifth factor is concerned with whether they are more concerned with *grammar and punctuation*, than with *spelling*.

It will be remembered that the first factor accounted for well over twice the percentage variance of any of the other factors. Now the first factor was concerned with teachers' practices, the other four factors being mainly concerned with attitudes. This would emphasize that it is what a teacher does in class, not what she says or thinks, that counts. However, these attitudes tend to cloud the factor analysis so another analysis was carried out omitting attitudes and just dealing with teachers' practices. In this analysis the factors emerging were, in this order, testing organization, time spent on spelling, rationality of approach, interest factor, and a final factor related to teachers' use of children's own vocabulary in the teaching of spelling. These are five areas in teaching behaviour, areas which necessarily overlap, but which reflect the various emphases in different schools and classes on creative writing and spelling.

Table 21 *Factor Analysis One*

Loadings included where s = > 0.26

Factor 1	s	Factor 2	s	Factor 3	s	Factor 4	s	Factor 5	s
+ Teacher's grade	0.77	Attitude to output	0.95	Attitude to vividness	0.86	Attitude to Hand-writing	0.91	Attitude to Grammar and Punctuation	0.75
Total time spent	0.74			Socio-economic status	0.33				
Frequency of testing	0.68			Organization of testing	0.3				
Time spent testing	0.67								
Organization of testing	0.65								
Mean percentage progress	0.61								
Time spent on lists	0.56								
Corrections practice	0.29								
– 'Year'	0.3	Attitude to Grammar and Punctuation	0.6	Consistency	0.54	Attitude to Spelling	0.67	Attitude to Spelling	0.28
		Attitude to Spelling	0.48	Attitude to Spelling	0.42				
% Variance = 16.5		% Variance = 7.4		% Variance = 6.9		% Variance = 6.8		% Variance = 4	
Teacher factor		Quantity/Quality		'Creative'/consistent approach		Appearance/Spelling		Grammar & Punctuation/Spelling	

Factor Analysis Two (excluding teacher's attitudes)

Factor 1	s	Factor 2	s	Factor 3	s	Factor 4	s	Factor 5	s
+ Teacher's grade	0.71	Time spent testing	0.78	'Corrections' practice	0.77	Time spent on lists	0.69	Time on Creative writing	0.66
Organization of testing	0.67	Total time spent	0.72	Mean percentage progress	0.48	Total time	0.47		
Frequency of testing	0.64	Teacher's grade	0.33	Teacher's grade	0.4	Teacher prepared lists	0.4		
Time spent testing	0.29	Time spent on lists	0.32			Frequency of testing	0.37		
		Teaching printed lists	0.31			Organization of testing	0.37		
		Mean percentage progress	0.28						
				Teaching printed lists	0.58			Asked for lists	0.59
								Mean percentage progress	0.41
% Variance = 13.14		% Variance = 12.68		% Variance = 10.85		% Variance = 9.46		% Variance = 9.15	
Testing Organization		Time spent on spelling		Rationality of approach		Verbal interest		Whether teachers use children's own vocabulary	

A stepwise regression analysis was next performed with mean actual progress as the dependent variable and subsequently with mean percentage progress as the dependent variable. In both analyses it was quite clear that the most important element was the 'year' that these 65 teachers were teaching, the penultimate or the final primary school year. In the case of mean actual progress 44%, and in the case of mean percentage progress 40% of the variation was due to the 'year' being taught. Irrespective of the year the teacher's grade was of definite importance (11% in mean actual progress and 4% in mean percentage progress). Other things being equal the total time spent on spelling was of great importance in considering mean percentage progress and all other things being equal, the use of printed word lists was seen to be detrimental.

Since the 'year' in which the teachers found themselves clouded the picture it seemed appropriate to repeat the regression analyses for the third and fourth years separately. The results of the two were different and indicate the different bias in teaching in the penultimate from the final primary school year.

In the third year the teacher's grade is of great importance 30% (mean actual progress) and 35% (mean percentage progress). Irrespective of this, time spent on instruction is the next important feature. Apart from this it is the mean S.E.S. level which determines actual progress, in other words the lower the social background level of the children, the greater the actual progress. Other things being equal, however, lists of words asked for by children and teacher prepared lists are the way in to actual spelling progress. For higher mean percentage progress in the third year, irrespective of teacher's grade, the total time spent on spelling is of definite importance and other things being equal, printed word lists are shown to be positively detrimental. It is possible that use of printed lists might seem to excuse teachers from further responsibilities in the teaching of spelling.

However, in the fourth year it is the time spent on testing that determines spelling progress—the total time spent in the case of actual progress, but the time spent on testing in the case of percentage progress. So it would appear that in the third year, the penultimate primary school year, classes which progress most in spelling do so because they have efficient and rational teachers. Irrespective of teacher efficiency, however, it seems to be time spent on spelling, particularly on instruction (i.e., study of word structure) that is important. Irrespective again of teacher and time spent, it would seem that those who teach from lists of words the children ask for in the course of their own writing or that they prepare themselves from children's needs, are most successful in teaching spelling unlike those who use the printed lists. Such lists indeed may well provide an easy alternative for the less linguistically sophisticated teacher. And in the final primary school year it is the amount of time spent on testing which is the major contribution to percentage spelling progress.

(c) *Summary of Results*

Examination of the teacher variables shows that there is greater attention to spelling during the penultimate primary school year, and it is quite clear that in relation to mean actual and mean percentage class progress, teachers' grade of tech-

Table 22 *Regression Analyses Teacher Variable*

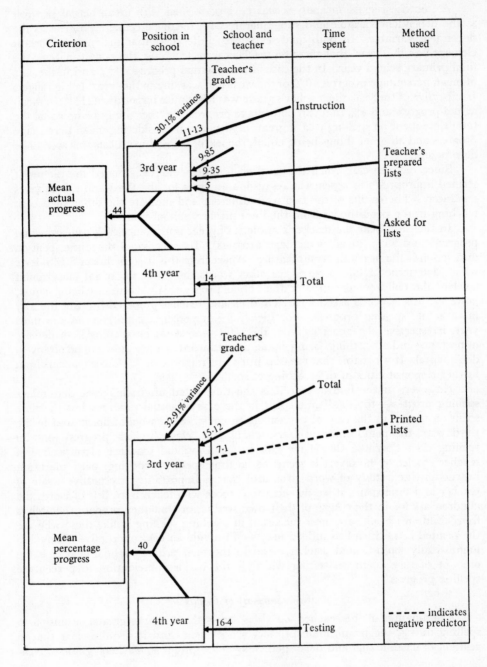

nical skill was of definite importance. Teachers' grades had been indexed by consistency of policy, regular and systematic testing, using marking as an occasion for teaching and exacting of corrections from children in a rational rather than a rote manner.

Time spent on spelling was important. In the third year it was time spent on instruction that contributed to attainment, and total time spent on spelling that led to mean percentage progress. This suggests that with the less favoured, time spent on *all* aspects of spelling (i.e., the testing of words and practising writing words) is important as well as time spent on instruction, i.e., the drawing of the attention of children to word structure. Indeed, in the fourth year percentage progress (highlighting the less favoured) is dependent on time spent, particularly on testing.

Teaching of spelling by lists acquired in the course of the children's free writing clearly influences actual progress, while the use of printed lists is seen to be detrimental to percentage progress.

It is quite clear from the evidence that the teacher's role is vital, and that if the teacher is rational and systematic in the teaching of spelling, using, directly or indirectly, words the children ask for in their writing, competence in spelling can be achieved by those linguistically less favoured.

V The influence of reading methods on spelling

1. *Outline of Previous Research*

The specific research reported in this chapter grew out of the growing belief at the Cambridge Institute of Education's Remedial Centre in the need to supplement remedial reading by an intensive course in spelling if retarded children are to be effectively assimilated into normal school streams. Schonell (1942) holds that spelling attainment depends less on children's linguistic background than on school experiences, and among school experiences, the activity of reading might well be expected to be an important influence. In the early years of the century, the rejection of the phonic method as a way of teaching reading was supported in the interests of spelling. Gill (1912) attributed reversals to phonic teaching, showing that the sentence method produced spelling efficiency, at least equal to that produced by phonic teaching. Horn (1919) agreed that the phonic method seemed to present no advantage in learning to spell, and Hilderbrandt (1923) pointed out the danger of stressing phonetic elements rather than viewing the word as a group of significant parts or as a whole. Forty years on, however, phonics were back in favour (Beltramo, 1954). Horn (1960) noted the growing interest in the possibility that phonic instruction may contribute to spelling ability. In the Michigan research (Anderson, 1965) it is shown that the most common mis-spellings of the English and Scottish samples were more often phonetic in nature and more readable than those of the American samples at all ages. This, Ewing (1965) suggests might be attributed to the differences in emphasis in reading method on the two sides of the Atlantic. Such suggestions would seem to justify the examination of the hypothesis that different methods of teaching reading give rise to different kinds of spelling errors.

2. *Method of Investigation*

The general method of the enquiry was to match pairs of children, who had learned to read using different methods and different media of teaching, and then to compare their ability in spelling.

Two separate experiments were set up.

Experiment 1

In the first experiment, 69 8-year-old children from a school using a rigorous phonic method were matched with children from a school using an equally rigorous look-and-say method. They were matched for sex, age, socio-economic level, and scores on N.F.E.R. Primary Verbal 1 and Raven's Progressive Matrices (1956).

The following tests were applied to the children:

1. The Graded Spelling Test from the Standard Reading Tests (Daniels and Diack, 1958).

2. A diagnostic dictation (Appendix A).

In this dictation, 75 % of the words occurred in Burrough's (1957) first 500 words in his study of the vocabulary of 5–6½-year-old children. 96% words in the story prepared were to be found in Burrough's complete list. 86% were comparable in difficulty with words spelt correctly by children with a spelling age of 8+. Of the phonic combinations introduced 93% conformed to rule. This gave opportunity for children to use their knowledge of rules or spelling precedent, also to see where children offer reasonable phonic alternatives, or where they produce phonic alternatives not conforming to rule. There were 7% grapho-phonemically irregular words.

The diagnostic test scripts were analysed using conventional error categories— Omissions and Contractions, Insertions, Transpositions, Doubling, Substitutions, Homophones, Perseverations and Unclassified (Spache 1940, Livingston 1961), except in the case of 'substitutions,' which are broken down into consonant and vowel substitution of letters, substitution with reasonable phonic alternatives and substitution of phonic alternatives not conforming to rule. These two latter categories were included as it seemed possible that here might appear the effect of training in reading. The criterion for inclusion in the column 'Reasonable phonic alternative' was conformity with precedent. The category "errors suggesting faulty auditory perception" was added to include words incorrectly perceived or encoded.

Results of Experiment 1.   Number of errors in each group were calculated and found to be very close in overall total, namely 1595 for look-and-say and 1550 for the phonic group. The greatest difference was between the reasonable phonic alternatives, of which the 69 children in the phonic group made 149, the 69 children in the look-and-say group 89 (p = <0.01) (the phonic alternatives not conforming to rule, being the same for both groups); the phonic group made only 31 unclassifiable errors, as against 103 in the look-and-say group (p = <0.01).

The results, cross-classified with respect to sex and I.Q., are shown in Table 1. Each child was classified according to the number of errors that he made in the two error categories that showed the greatest difference, viz., reasonable phonic alternatives and unclassified errors, and the resulting distributions were compared using the Kolmogorov-Smirnov two-sample test (Siegel 1956). Due to the smallness of the matched sub-samples, only one comparison exceeds the 5% level of significance. But, *within* the 85–115 I.Q. range, the other comparisons show consistent trends. If a gross comparison is made between all 69 children in the look-and-say group and all 69 children in the phonic group, it turns out that their results differ beyond the 1% level of significance in each error category.

For the group with the higher (116+) I.Q., it is instructive to note that differences due to different teaching methods vanish almost completely. Over both I.Q. ranges, the girls show a slight overall superiority over the boys. No data are available for children in the 'below 85' I.Q. range.

In addition to comparing the frequencies with which particular kinds of error occur, we can also check on the different ways in which the errors are inter-related. We can, for example, enquire whether the tendency to select reasonable phonic alternatives is associated with the tendency to select homophones. If we find that two kinds of error tend to go together, we can then ask whether the inter-correlation is higher among one group than the other. Some gross measures of inter-correlation have been calculated, and the following pattern emerges.

61

Table 23 *Comparison of Mean Error Scores for Two Matched Samples Taught by Phonic and Look-and-Say Methods*

Error Category			I.Q. (85–115) Mean No. Errors per Child		Signif. level of Diff.		I.Q. (116+) Mean No. Errors per Child		Signif. level of Diff.
		n	L. & S.	Phonic		n	L. & S.	Phonic	
Reasonable Phonic Alternative	Boys	26	1.31	2.85	p<0.025	9	1.44	1.11	n.s.
	Girls	25	1.32	2.40	n.s.	9	1.00	0.56	n.s.
	X̄		1.31	2.63	p<0.025		1.22	0.83	n.s.
Unclassified Errors	Boys	26	2.19	0.35	n.s.	9	Nil	Nil	n.s.
	Girls	25	1.84	0.88	n.s.	9	Nil	Nil	n.s.
	X̄		2.02	0.61	n.s.		Nil	Nil	n.s.

Among the look-and-say group, the highest comparative correlation is between transposition of letters and vowel substitutions. Among the phonic group, the highest correlation is between reasonable phonic alternatives and homophones. Both these correlations exceed the 2% level of significance.

Experiment 2

Having compared two methods of teaching reading and their influence on spelling ability, approaches to reading via two different alphabets were studied. 115 children learning to read in traditional orthography (t.o.) by rigorous look-and-say and phonic schemes, were compared with 115 children taught to read using the initial teaching alphabet (i.t.a.).

The look-and-say and phonic samples were compared with the i.t.a. samples with confidence since all three samples had been taught rigorously by teachers (and not only teachers but also head teachers) who were totally committed to the method used, heavily prejudiced against other methods, and whose schools were much visited as exponents of these methods. All samples were from schools in working class areas, largely council house property.

One-hundred-and-fifteen pairs were studied, matched for sex, age (within one month) socio-economic status and scores on Moray House 1A and Raven's Progressive Matrices (1956).

Results of Experiment 2.   Numbers of errors in each group were found to be very close in overall total, namely 3,163 for i.t.a., and 3,059 for t.o. There is a difference at p<0.001 in the single for double letter error, and in the substitution of reasonable phonic alternatives and in homophones, indicating significantly more errors in i.t.a.

62

than in t.o., in all three error categories the mean for i.t.a. being greater but the variance less than in t.o. The difference between t.o. and i.t.a. in faulty auditory perception, perseveration, and unclassified errors, shows significantly more errors in t.o. than in i.t.a. again p<0.001.

Table 24 *Comparison of Mean Error Scores for Two Matched Samples Taught by Different Media (t.o. and i.t.a.)*

Error Category			(85–115) Mean No. Errors per Child		Signif. level of Diff.	(116+) Mean No. Errors per Child			Signif. level of Diff.
		n	i.t.a.	t.o.		n	i.t.a.	t.o.	
Single for Double	Boys	33	3.24	2.03	p<0.005	21	1.76	1.33	n.s.
	Girls	43	2.65	1.28	p<0.005	18	0.83	0.56	n.s.
	X̄		2.91	1.61	p<0.001		1.33	0.97	n.s.
Reasonable phonic Alternative	Boys	33	2.94	1.70	p<0.005	21	1.76	1.24	n.s.
	Girls	43	2.37	1.44	p<0.025	18	1.22	1.11	n.s.
	X̄		2.62	1.55	p<0.001		1.51	1.18	n.s.
Faulty Auditory Perception	Boys	33	1.91	4.55	p<0.05	21	0.67	2.24	n.s.
	Girls	43	2.02	3.12	n.s.	18	0.56	1.89	n.s.
	X̄		1.97	3.74	p<0.05		0.62	2.08	p<0.025
Homophones	Boys	33	1.15	0.30	p<0.005	21	0.19	0.29	n.s.
	Girls	43	0.86	0.47	n.s.	18	0.28	0.17	n.s.
	X̄		0.99	0.39	p<0.01		0.23	0.23	n.s.
Perseveration	Boys	33	0.06	0.18	n.s.	21	Nil	0.05	n.s.
	Girls	43	Nil	0.54	n.s.	18	Nil	0.06	n.s.
	X̄		0.03	0.38	n.s.		Nil	0.05	n.s.
Unclassified errors	Boys	33	0.58	3.30	p<0.05	21	Nil	0.86	n.s.
	Girls	43	1.00	2.86	p<0.025	18	Nil	Nil	n.s.
	X̄		.82	3.05	p<0.001		Nil	.46	n.s.

As before, rough measures of association were obtained to gauge the extent to which different kinds of error clustered together. It was found that the chief cluster with respect to i.t.a. was concerned with:

1. Substitution of reasonable phonic alternatives.
2. Homophones.
3. Single for double letter substitutions.

In the cases t.o., the main cluster was with respect to:

1. Transposition of syllables.
2. Perseveration, and
3. Faulty auditory perception.

A systematic breakdown of these results, by sex and I.Q., is shown in Table 2. The distributions of appropriate sub-samples were compared by the Kolmogorov-Smirov two-sample test. Once again, the girls tend to be slightly superior to the boys, and differences due to the different teaching media (i.t.a. and t.o.), are mostly reduced to non-significance in the higher I.Q. range.

The errors associated in t.o. are errors of inexactitude, viz., transposed syllables, syllables running on, syllables incorrectly perceived or incorrectly encoded, and words that are unclassifiable. i.t.a. children thus attack spelling more systematically, evidence being:

1. Fewer unclassified errors.
2. Fewer perseverations.
3. Fewer transpositions of syllables.
4. Fewer errors suggesting faulty auditory perception or encoding.

On the other hand, there are specific spelling problems, e.g., more single letters where these should be double, a spelling convention that is rational though unexpected, and this in spite of the fact that i.t.a. children have been deliberately and of necessity taught spelling rules, e.g., 'no' instead of 'know'. Indeed, frequently the more sophisticated i.t.a. taught children fall over backwards and present 'tide' in preference to 'tied' which is extremely close to the i.t.a. 'tied'!

It would seem that i.t.a. taught children, with their more systematic and economical attack, present a more receptive base for the teaching of spelling conventions.

3. *Trends Suggested by Experiments 1 and 2*

Livingston (1961) demonstrated similarity in pattern of errors with Masters' (1937) American investigation. Each group in the present study follows a similar pattern though the percentage of insertions is lower in every group while the percentages of omissions and unclassified spellings, are higher. With these exceptions (probably due to differences in classification), the group which compares most nearly with Livingston's is the i.t.a. group, though this group shows a higher percentage of homophones than Livingston's since Scottish children differentiate homophones orally, e.g., 'tied' and 'tide.' Indeed, it is in this particular error category that the trend from few errors in look-and-say, through phonic, to most in i.t.a. is most evident.

Table 25 *Comparative Frequency of Errors for Each of Three Teaching Systems*

	Teaching System		
Frequency	Look-and-Say	Phonic	i.t.a.
High	6, 7, 8	11	1, 2, 3, 4, 5
Medium	9, 10, 11	1, 2, 3, 4, 5, 6, 7, 8	9, 10, 11
Low	1, 2, 3, 4, 5	9, 10	6, 7, 8

1 Doubling (Single for Double, Double for Single)
2 Substitution of consonants
3 Non-conforming phonic alternatives
4 Faulty auditory perceptions
5 Homophones
6 Omissions
7 Insertions
8 Perseveration
9 Transpositions
10 Substitution of vowels
11 Reasonable phonic alternatives

This trend can be seen from a study of the ranking of methods according to the percentage of errors in each category (Table 25). It will be seen that i.t.a. comes off best only in categories of error arising from lack of economy and control of output, viz., omissions, insertions and perseverations.

It will be seen that where the phonic method is superior is in producing fewer transpositions and fewer substitutions of vowels. Also when a major substitution is made by phonic children, it is more often a reasonable phonic alternative. The look-and-say method produces, as one would expect, much better visual attack. There are fewest doubling errors (both single for double and double for single), fewest consonant substitutions, fewest non-conforming phonic alternatives, fewest errors of faulty auditory perception and fewest homophones. It can also be seen that in all but three error categories the two methods and the initial teaching alphabet lie on a continuum from look-and-say through phonic to i.t.a. The strength of look-and-say lies in consonantal exactness, superior attempts at overall structuring, and better semantic association (e.g., in homophones where the visual aspect of the word is conjured up directly by the meaning and associations of the word). Between this and the economy and discipline of i.t.a., at the other end of the continuum, lies the phonic method, with neither fewest nor most errors in any of the above categories, yet superior in the remaining ones of fewest transpositions, fewest substitutions of vowels and the greatest number of reasonable phonic alternatives (a 'good' error).

There appear to be important implications here for remedial teaching. For children who are finding spelling difficult, those taught originally by a look-and-say method are restricted with visual but no rational reference, those taught by phonic methods are able to make a reasonable attempt which may well be a homophone, while i.t.a. children have the sort of non-redundant 'skeletal' structure from which conventional English spellings can be readily developed.

4. *Conclusion*

The use of one of two reading methods (look-and-say or phonic) or a new medium (i.t.a.), when rigorously operated, does not seem to affect the level of spelling attainment.

Differences in method or medium seem, however, to lead to differences in perception which show themselves in the type of spelling error made.

VI

A. Discussion of the Molar Analysis of Spelling

The results of the investigation not only indicate certain specific approaches and types of teaching behaviour, but seem to point to where we stand in the incidental/systematic controversy. It is clear that favoured children, children with good verbal intelligence, who have acquired certain abilities such as good visual perception of word forms with all its inter-correlated attributes, who are of high socio-economic status and favourable family order and size, tend to learn to spell without much difficulty.

It is clear that those who are ill-favoured in these respects progress in spelling, provided that they are given good teaching. Good teaching implies a rational, consistent, systematic approach to teaching. It implies willingness on the part of the teacher to spend time on instruction, and, while marking, time on pointing out the internal structure of words. The good teacher is, in fact, training visual perception of word forms, an ability that the favoured child acquired before the age of nine.

There emerges from this investigation an area of good teaching of this particular skill that is at odds with the traditional picture of the way spelling is taught in English schools. 'The traditional spelling lesson is an ad hoc approach to the task of inter-nationalization (of spelling patterns) and one which, for lack of awareness of the working of the orthography, falls back on random procedures and on rote learning' (Mackay and Thompson, 1968, 68). It has been shown in this investigation, the extent to which this obtains in a sample of 65 classes in primary schools. The writer has shown that haphazard practices have no part in the acquisition of the code, or, in the terminology of MacKay and Thompson, in successfully internalizing the model, but that where rational teaching procedures are followed, the code is indeed learned, and becomes automatized.

The attributes mentioned above, correlated with visual perception of word form, and intercorrelated, depend on use of language. Fundamental to *verbal intelligence* is speech, and it is obvious that without language facility, however attentively children may be inveigled into looking at words about them, they will not improve in the particular kind of *visual perception* that is essential to learning to spell, since, as was shown in Chapter Two, the more familiar children are with words the more likely they are to see them as a whole (Howes and Solomon, 1951).

Carefulness of handwriting which determines legibility, and *speed of handwriting* depend on the opportunity and motivation to write. So does *fluency* in creative writing. *Auditory perception* (which, though a member of this inter-correlated complex, does not seem to be in any way a strong determinant of spelling ability) depends on clear articulation of language in the conversation and story telling of adults.

Generalizing ability, both at nine and at ten is, in the analysis, a minor predictor of spelling ability. It is looking at word forms, e.g., discriminating between and comparing words, that occurs when teachers instruct, and time spent on this is the most predictive teaching variable, after teacher's grade, in the regression analysis of mean actual progress. Examination of the effect on children's generalizing ability when no spelling teaching of any kind occurred, suggested that generalizing ability which implies a qualitative change in spelling behaviour occurs for most children in the junior school, and is dependent on rational and systematic teaching procedures.

What determines this qualitative change? It is a change that has not occurred in an eleven year old child who writes 'infuasem' for 'enthusiasm', whereas another eleven year old child writes 'imfuseasumn'. Both derive from auditory or articulatory faults, but, in the latter 'in' and 'fuse' are quite reasonable alternatives, and the final syllable clearly reflects the final syllable of autumn, a familiar letter sequence. It is a change which will be discussed later in connection with molecular analysis of the skill. At the moment we are concerned with sifting information from the molar study which can be of practical value to teachers. It is therefore worth summarizing the ways in which rational teaching procedures can effect this qualitative change.

1. It has been shown that when children are taught to read by a rule-following method, their spelling errors consist of reasonable (according to spelling precedent) as opposed to unreasonable alternatives.

2. It is evident that children whose attention is directed by their teacher, by rational correction practice, to structural resemblances in words, improve their spelling competence, which, by definition, means they acquire generalizing ability.

3. Children with swift motor control of handwriting write groups of letters in connected form, sparked off by a phoneme which they articulate sub-vocally. This would suggest that what is needed is practice in the swift writing of familiar words, not copying, but with the multi-sensory backing advocated by Fernald (1943).

4. Familiar words, for example children's names, names of months, seasons, roads, towns, advertised products, etc., set in motion serial probability. The word is heard or imaged, and reconstructed in the light of the known word, e.g., 'high draw lick' for 'hydraulic'. Such independently correct, but conjointly incorrect sequences are inevitably etymologically incorrect. It would need a knowledge not only of the meaning of 'hydraulic' but of classical roots to attack this correctly, unseen. But gradually, one letter string at a time, familiarization takes place, e.g., in learning that adjectives frequently end in 'ic' not 'ick'. It is inevitably gradual. The probability of such sequences coming together correctly increases as the rational teaching procedures summarized above are followed. But this is fundamental to the molecular study of the nature of the skill, to which we must now proceed.

B. Discussion of the Molecular Analysis of Spelling arising from Previous Results

So far, concern has been with analysis of gross variables in learning to spell. It was thought that an investigation like this should not end without raising questions of a more refined sort about what children actually learn when they learn to spell. If one were clear about this, the problem of the most fruitful methods of teaching children would be greatly simplified.

How does the information available about (a) intrinsic characteristics in children that determine spelling ability, (b) methods of teaching that produce such ability, supplement what is already known about the nature of the skill, and what questions remain to be answered? It has been demonstrated quite clearly that spelling ability is 'caught', concurrently with other linguistic skills by certain favoured children, but that others, who are not so favoured, achieve the skill only after a considerable amount of rational, systematic, teaching. In addition the negative results from the examination of the influence of maturation tend to confirm the main conclusion of the research which shows the importance of the teaching variables.

The implication of the findings about the child variables is, that spelling ability depends on at least three major constituents:

(i) Verbal ability
(ii) Visuo-perceptual ability
(iii) Perceptuo-motor ability

The question for any molecular analysis of spelling is to get clearer how the three constituents enter into the complex skill of spelling. To call spelling a skill may seem to prejudge the issue; for is not the ideal which any teacher hopes to achieve that children should emerge with a settled habit to spell correctly and does not Schonell's description of spelling make it sound very much like a habit?

To make such an antithesis, however, between skills and habits is to misunderstand these concepts. We call something a habit, for instance, hitting a tennis ball low over the net into the opposite court, when the player tends to repeat this action and when it is the sort of action that he can do automatically, i.e., without giving his mind to it at the moment that he does it. This same action, however, could also be called a skill if we wish to draw attention to the intelligent and effective co-ordination of movements to bring about this specific end which the player had in mind. Also, this particular action could be regarded as intelligent if it was conceived in the context of defeating the opponent who was on the opposite side of the court. It is important also for a player who is concentrating mainly on placing the ball where his opponent is not, to have mastered a whole repertoire of skills which function for him as lower-order habits in the context of the game seen as being concerned with defeating his opponent. Just because we call something a habit, it does not mean that it need not involve skill or that the action so described could not be regarded as skilful in some other context.

When we turn to spelling, therefore, the fact that it functions as a habit in a wider context such as creative writing is not inconsistent with its being a skill if we wish to draw attention to the intelligence which may be displayed in spelling if the child has in mind the limited objective of getting the word right. The crucial question to ask is what are the elements which he has to see as a means of bringing about this end, or what specific constituent strategies does he have to master in order to bring about this end. This is particularly important for teaching; for if we want to teach children to spell rationally, we must know to what their attention must be directed and what they must practise. Also, even with good spellers for whom spelling has become a habit, there must be something to which they can direct their attention when what Schonell calls 'the hitch' occurs. We must therefore, look for these elements which make spelling a skill and which are essential for teaching in the three areas that seem to be indicated by the molar analysis.

1. *Verbal Ability*

In the regression analysis, *verbal intelligence* was clearly shown to be the factor most predictive of spelling ability. It accounted for more than half the variance at 9 and at 11 years. This is supported by the Swedish investigation (Ahlstrom, 1965) into the structure of spelling ability, a factor analysis from which the first factor emerged as a high *verbal factor*. This involved language training, for example familiarity with words, their structure and their use. This was the verbal factor which Townsend (1947) spotted when she showed the correlation between spelling and vocabulary to be higher than that between spelling and reading comprehension or spelling and tests of academic aptitude. Indeed it is only to be expected that word enthusiasts are able to spell well, whether their enthusiasm stems from etymology, trained eloquence or cross-word puzzles. The Swedish analysis showed skill in reading and spelling to be related to each other, but some aspects of reading to be more closely related to spelling than others, particularly reading aloud, e.g., 'Reading aloud seems to be associated with skill in spelling, since in principle at least it is possible to read and spell words correctly without having any idea of their meaning.' (Ahlstrom, 1965, 37). Reading aloud entails the auditory analysis which is essential to spelling. It also associates the look of the word with the articulated and heard sound of the word. Articulation itself is helped and hence spelling, since children with a very poor spoken language tend to be bad spellers. (Schonell, 1942).

A further relevant factor is one which appears in the Swedish analysis as 'an intellectual factor of an inductive nature'. Since this is not merely a 'verbal intelligence factor', it may be helpful to look at this 'intellectual factor of an inductive nature' more broadly. It is, in the light of previous discussion, obvious that to be aware of the rationale of English spelling takes a child a long way to being able to spell. It will be remembered that children, taught to read in a rule-following manner by a pure phonic method, not only continue to spell in a reasonable manner, making when uncertain, reasonable phonic alternatives rather than haphazard shots at a word, but also look on written language as something fairly reasonable. Is it far fetched to suggest that such an outlook is conducive to working inductively, and that the intellectual factor of an inductive nature drawn out in factor analysis by the Swedes, can be more readily tapped by individuals who look on written language as a reasonable and manageable medium? A final factor in the Swedish analysis is an 'interest in reading factor' deriving from attitude to books and book borrowing habits. In this factor is loaded word-identification which, it is to be expected, is a characteristic of the fast and avid reader.

The cluster of significant correlations around verbal abilities associated with socio-economic status, the fact that verbal intelligence is negatively associated with percentage progress in spelling, i.e., highlighting those children who begin at a low attainment level, but markedly progress, the fact that family order is a small but positive predictor of percentage progress, are all reminders that spelling ability is influenced by verbal experience. This may be the case because it is the norm for parents of high socio-economic status to talk, and to read to children, thereby attending to word structure, or because a child is in the favoured position as an only or eldest child and hence inevitably at the receiving end of 'talk'. If 'talk' determines so many linguistic skills, not least spelling, the question is being posed and bravely faced in compensatory education, not only of the necessity of talking with young children, but of how to achieve this talking within the large class and with children unaccustomed to variable, exploratory and mutually satisfying talk.

The conclusion of the results of study of the teaching variable show that, to achieve spelling ability, less favoured children need to be taught, and taught rationally and systematically. If their attention is constantly drawn to details of word structure, similarities of letter sequence, and the varying probabilities of such sequences (something which the more favoured children acquire incidentally) if this is linked with oracy and in the cause of creative writing, the less favoured children may not only improve in the verbal skills such as spelling, but thereby improve in what is called, in this study, verbal intelligence.

2. *Visuo-perceptual Ability*

In the analysis reported in Chapter Three, the next most powerful predictor of spelling ability, after *verbal intelligence* was *visual perception of word form*. This, in the test situation, showed children's ability to reproduce briefly exposed words, words unlikely to be known semantically to the children, but words containing common letter sequences. This demanded verbal flexibility of the kind discussed in the last section under *verbal ability* since this is a necessary constituent of the ability to reconstitute a word mentally after brief tachistoscopic exposure (which is presumably what happens when a word 'springs to mind' in an individual's composing of a sentence). This reconstitution is automatized. Yet if the child is asked to spell orally, the child can read it off from sequences of part-perceptions of visual imagery, or by auditory syllabic fragmentation.

To be able to reconstitute a word seen fleetingly involves:

   (i)   being able to 'read' the word
  (ii) being able to recall the 'read' word
 (iii) having recalled the first letter/string of letters, to reconstruct the rest, letter after letter or letter sequence after letter sequence
 (iv) being able to encode graphemically

This in fact, is equivalent to the factor in the Swedish analysis called *immediate memory for visual material*, and there is considerable supporting evidence of its importance. Hartmann (1931) it will be remembered, showed that good spellers were distinguished by their immediate memory span for meaningful visual stimuli. In this study, visual perception of word form was strongly predictive of spelling attainment at nine and at eleven years, but was negatively associated with percentage progress (in other words with those who made most progress from a low initial level). This again suggests that the ability to fixate and then retain and reconstitute a word is something acquired by more favoured children in the early years, but that lack of this ability can be supplemented or compensated for by good teaching. For time spent on instruction (i.e., attention to word structure) was a powerful predictor of mean actual progress in the teaching variable. In addition, children receiving no spelling teaching deteriorated rather than improved in rational attack in conformity with spelling precedent, an activity which clearly necessitates visual perception of word form

What then is revealed in this factor that contributes to our knowledge of the nature of the spelling process?

1. Efficient visual preception of word form is acquired by favoured children (i.e., it is strongly associated with other linguistic abilities).

2. It can be supplemented or compensated for, when children are taught to pay attention to word structure.

3. Among favoured children, and this includes children taught to read by a rule-following procedure, it is a front-line strategy when habitual spelling breaks down. (This fact can be inferred from the study of generalizing processes at nine and ten years.)

4. Efficient visual perception of word form is a necessary pre-requisite to reconstitution of a long word briefly exposed.

These conclusions about the importance of the components of visual perception in spelling have been drawn from the molar analysis. Confirmation of them seems to be forthcoming from a particular exercise conducted in order to examine the role of serial probability in learning to spell.

Teachers usually accept that if spelling is a necessary skill it is a skill which has to be learned. Yet when faced with the question of generalization of letter sequence through knowledge of serial probability, they begin to talk about maturation and cognitive levels of development, forgetting that this generalization is not on a conscious logical plane but at a mechanical, imaginal, kinaesthetic level. In good spellers this is automatized, though in remedial spelling less favoured children have to be made aware of the mechanisms of generalization before it becomes automatized.

Earlier in Chapter Two mention was made of an analysis of children's spelling, at 10 years, of the word 'saucer' (data in appendix C). It is probable that many of these children had never written the word before. This then was a useful word to consider in connection with serial probability. How do children come to write the word 'saucer' correctly, never having learned to spell it, written it nor perhaps even read it?

It is useful to examine the alternatives offered by the children and the frequency with which they are offered. The most frequently presented alternative is 'sauser' (presented 67 times, i.e., 7%), a very reasonable alternative. The vowel combinations are correct; only the internal consonant has been substituted. The next most frequent alternatives are 'suacer' and 'sorser', both offered 23 times. The word 'suacer' contains a vowel transposition, a visual error often made by children who do not look carefully at words. On the other hand 'sorser' could come about in several ways. It could derive from faulty auditory perception. The child hears the spoken word in a distorted way and reproduces this. Usually this is incorrect. Only once in the 967 children did faulty auditory perception produce some structural resemblance within a not only reasonable, but even poetically acceptable alternative when the phrase 'flowing shower' was offered in place of 'flying saucer'!

It is more likely, however, that the distortion occurs later in the process. The word may be heard correctly but either visualized or, more probably, repeated sub-vocally with distorted articulation (e.g., 'altimeter' written 'outimetre'. As is to be expected, the auditorily distorted alternative 'sorser' occurs more often among children in the lower socio-economic levels. Even, however, if 'sorser' derived entirely from faulty articulation, this leaves as alternatives 121 consonant substitutions, 57 omissions, 23 inversions, 18 single vowel substitutions, none of which would seem to be of auditory or articulatory origin. These would seem to be visuo-motor errors and the answer would seem to lie in knowledge of serial probability. For each word (indeed for each child at any point in time) there is a probability level. These probabilities can be grouped—so that we can say from the evidence that there is a fairly equal chance that a ten year old will spell the word 'saucer' correctly or incorrectly. If incorrect, there is a one in seven chance that he will write a very reasonable alternative, e.g., 'sauser', a one in three chance that he will make a fairly reasonable alternative, and fairly even chances that it will be reasonable or unreasonable. These words lie on a probability continuum from correct to highly bizarre, e.g., saucer—sauser—sacer—scous—splenace.

What causes the child to write the correct word? It is tempting to write 'make the correct choice'—but is there an element of selection? Sometimes indeed there is. The child hesitates; the pencil is poised; he may write, check visually and correct what he has written. The competent adult, faced with a new and difficult word to write may go through the same hesitancy pattern. Rather as the adult or competent reader goes into reserve technique, and analyses in phonics when reading at sight and held up with a new and difficult word, so the writer, faced with a difficult word to write, hesitates, and tries it out by a new strategy. But the task here is not analysis and synthesis of learned sight-sound associations which can rarely be other than they are, but a selection from several alternatives, 's-au', 'aw?', 'or?' superficially all of equal possibility. It is only the sophisticated writer who would know that 's' with a suffix 'cer' would be followed by 'au' not 'aw'. This could be called a rule, but such rules could only be formulated as such by a sophisticated writer, who might then apply it to particular instances. After many such applications, a habit of following such a rule might be set up, emerging as what Schonell calls a machine-like movement when words 'flow from the end of our pen . . . engram complexes dependent for their stimuli upon dozens of muscles which have been co-ordinated with definite strength, sequence, accuracy and rapidity.' (Schonell, 1942, 278). For the poor speller, the hesitancy routine provides further uncertainty, since without 'rules' he cannot select with certainty, in other words, he has not regularized any sequence of strategies.

As a skill, spelling is ultimately achieved by imitation, successive approximation, practice, and active self-testing, before the skill becomes a motor habit, with a reserve of appropriate tactical procedures when the habit fails. Writing the word 'saucer' the child images and articulates the word sub-vocally. Then according to his visual and motor experience he writes swiftly and the word may or may not be correct.

It is not so much as Fernald (1943) said, a curve of mastery for each word, but a curve of visuo-motor experience of writing a particular letter sequence, which may or may not be directly equivalent to one or more phonemes, heard or articulated. The more often the association between the articulated and heard sound (in relation to sounds immediately succeeding and preceding it), *and* the written sequence occurs, the greater the probability that this sequence will be repeatedly evoked in relation to the preceding and succeeding letter sequence.

3. *Perceptuo-motor Ability*

In the regression analysis of the child variable the third most predictive factor was the one termed *carefulness*, evinced in the quality of handwriting, the relevant criteria being well-formed, legible and barely legible handwriting. Now this might well suggest that children who are able to spell well at nine are, as they write carefully, deliberately and intelligently assessing the possible alternative strategies necessary to spelling as they write. But carefulness in writing is significantly correlated (.43) with speed of handwriting, which is indeed a subsequent predictor in the regression analysis. So these children who write carefully tend to write more swiftly. That casual and slow handwriting are correlated is of interest since there is here implied an uncertainty about letter formation and a time consuming uncertainty about letter sequence as well as letter formation. It is worth noting that slow speed of handwriting is the most important element in percentage progress (which highlights those children who begin at a very low attainment level but make most progress). It is more important than poor verbal intelligence or poor visual perception of word form. Speed of writing is clearly basic to spelling progress.

It is not possible to plumb the origin of this slowness. Speed of writing is correlated (.5) with verbal intelligence. But speed of writing is an aspect of a motor skill much more akin to walking or riding a bicycle than spelling is. Such skills are acquired through successive approximations to the most economic and effective movement, and learned through identification, imitation and practice. This, if anything, would seem to be an area within the teaching orbit. Writing, whether acquired through copying, or preferably finger-tracing a written reproduction (Fernald, 1943), would seem to be directly a contributory sub-skill of spelling, and indirectly of creative writing, that it is disastrous to neglect.

These, then, are the kind of elements which make spelling a skill, which constitute the kind of strategies undertaken when habitual spelling breaks down. These are the elements which, the molar analysis has shown, must be taught if spelling is indeed to become a habit, so that the individual can attend to the content of what he is writing.

VII Conclusion

Before spelling can become habitual, that is, completely automatized, it has to go through the process of skill learning. Spelling a word correctly may be a limited objective for a child, involving intelligent and adaptive use of strategies. Such strategies may have to be utilized when an habitually good speller is faced with a strange new word, and it is important to distinguish the types of strategy which a child can be taught to use.

It is possibly useful to consider the development of some of these strategies by constructing a simple flow chart.

Flow Chart of organisation of spelling behaviour

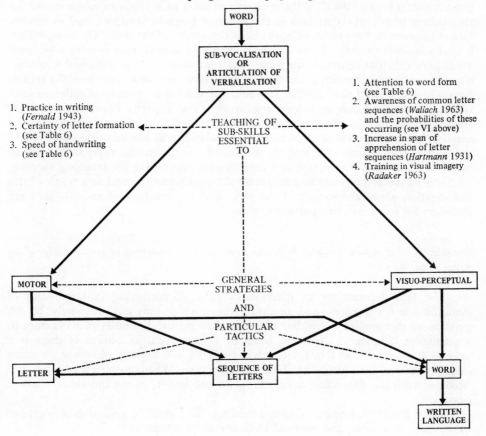

1. Practice in writing (*Fernald* 1943)
2. Certainty of letter formation (see Table 6)
3. Speed of handwriting (see Table 6)

1. Attention to word form (see Table 6)
2. Awareness of common letter sequences (*Wallach* 1963) and the probabilities of these occurring (see VI above)
3. Increase in span of apprehension of letter sequences (*Hartmann* 1931)
4. Training in visual imagery (*Radaker* 1963)

WORD

SUB-VOCALISATION OR ARTICULATION OF VERBALISATION

TEACHING OF SUB-SKILLS ESSENTIAL TO

GENERAL STRATEGIES AND PARTICULAR TACTICS

MOTOR

VISUO-PERCEPTUAL

LETTER

SEQUENCE OF LETTERS

WORD

WRITTEN LANGUAGE

But all this does is to demonstrate some alternatives in the form of strategies and tactics that are available between the ideational input and the written language, and suggestions as to the kind of teaching procedures that will foster such strategies. It is, however, not a matter of alternative strategies so much as range of strategies from effective to less effective and this cannot be brought out in such a chart. Nor can this kind of chart give weight to the sub-skills and conditions revealed in this and earlier investigations as necessary to these strategies. It cannot show the varying effects *within* teaching procedures, when, for example, a particular kind of spelling list is taught. It cannot show the varying effects *between* teaching procedures, according to whether lists are or are not taught, the nature of such lists, the frequency and organization of testing or the rationality of correction procedure. But a skill like spelling has been shown in this investigation not only to vary greatly according to how an individual is taught to spell, but also to a child's social and linguistic background. There is no possibility of reference in such a chart to variability of social and linguistic background. There can be no reference to personality variables (Holmes, 1959) or to the contribution of the vital 'self-image of oneself as a good speller' (Lecky, 1945). All the chart can do is to act as a heuristic device for the teacher which will alert him to the range of possible strategies, and to remind him of the current state of knowledge about the nature of the skill. The danger here is that a student or teacher, 'having understood the model, may remain convinced ever afterwards that he understands the reality as well' . . . 'mathematical formulae, graphs, and descriptive literature do not have quite the same danger as the replica type of model.' (McLeish, 1969). It would be possible to consider a different kind of model, one for example, attempting to show the disparity between the desired state of affairs and the observed state. This is the task of the informed and rational teacher, however, who is anxious to know to what extent her teaching objectives in the area of spelling are obtained by the actual techniques she uses; such a model could be relevant to that part of this investigation concerning the teaching variable.

It is therefore proposed to summarize the conclusions formed as a result of this investigation about the nature of the skill, and the teaching elements which are necessary for success in this particular skill.

Summary of what is seen, in the light of this investigation to contribute to our knowledge of the nature of the skill

The skill depends on an individual's habitual perceiving in large units of common letter sequences, and retaining these, which may not necessarily be dependent on meaningful words, but which are in a probability order of occurrence in a particular language. Until this becomes automatized, utilization of these is a priority strategy. Other strategies such as auditory/articulatory, phoneme encoding into graphemes, are available, but less effective. When automatized, the skill becomes habitual, depending upon the speed and quality of the individual's motor dexterity.

Apart from talk, being read to and reading, all of which in some degree engender interest in word form, the essential elements to be taught are:

1. awareness of common letter sequences, and the probabilities of these occurring;

2. the increase in the span of apprehension of letter sequences, which necessarily involves

3. the use of imagery;

4. certainty of formation of letters in writing;

5. swift handwriting;

Spelling is of no more use intrinsically than hopping or adding. Spelling is no use unless one wants to write, but to write without being able to spell would be to court circumlocution, to fail to express what one has to say with precision and to fail in fact to communicate. To this extent, it is a vital skill, and one which teachers must learn to teach as economically and efficiently as possible. Well before this investigation began, Richmond (1960) confirmed Horn (1954) in pointing out that adequate research is available for improving spelling instruction. Marksheffel (1964 182) adds, 'But the problem of *how* to get teachers to apply the findings of research, to their class-room practices remains'. The resurgence of interest in spelling through the work of people like Freyberg and Arvidsen, who advocate a positive and systematic approach to spelling and such people as Fries in Linguistics and Bruner and Wallach in coding systems, should solve the problem of how to get all these findings applied in the classroom. What this investigation adds, is that those children who do not learn to spell 'incidentally' can be, and indeed are being taught by the systematic practice of rational teachers in the cause of creative writing.

Appendices

APPENDIX A

(i) Tests and test construction
(ii) Questionnaires

2nd Year

1. LEFTHANDED WRITERS
2. GLASSES WORN
3. HEARING TEST ADMINISTERED

DICTATION

One day, as I was walking down Bridge Street, I heard the sound of trotting. I turned and saw behind me the shaggy dark hair of a frightened little horse. I searched in my pockets for an apple from my dinner to give him. 'I know where you should be,' I said. So I removed the belt of my raincoat and tied it around his neck and led him back. I opened the gate, and with satisfaction he galloped into his own field. I was certainly very happy that now he was safe, away from the noisy and dangerous traffic.

I expect you would like to know the little horse's name. Well, first of all I will tell you his mother's name. I am going to show it to you for a very short time and then hide it and ask you to write it from memory.

LOOK: 4 seconds. Write FLAGRANCY

Very few people know the pony's name, but I do. I will let you into the secret, but you must not start writing till I say 'GO' and hold up your pencils when I say 'STOP'.

LOOK: 3 seconds. Write: 10 seconds. VAGABOND

3rd Year

1. LEFTHANDED WRITERS
2. GLASSES WORN
3. HEARING TEST ADMINISTERED

DICTATION

Late one night my friend woke me saying 'Would you enjoy a trial-run in my new helicopter?'

I had scarcely scrambled into my track-suit before we were away. The lights of the city glowed beneath: the stars above. I was beginning to wonder about our destination when I caught sight of the spinning knife edge and the surface of what must have been a type of flying saucer whistling round us. We dodged skilfully to avoid an accident. To our relief, the space-craft regained height and we sank down to earth and the comfortable bed I had never actually left.

Look at these words (3 seconds). Write FRUIT, FIELD, LODGE.

Listen to these words. Write SUITABLE, BELIEF, HEDGE.

4th Year

PASSAGE 3

A peculiar shape was approaching from the southern valley. Gradually they distinguished a recently designed aeroplane circling above.

The machine touched down with precision in the rough mountainous region without even scraping its surface. The children surrounded the pilot who explained that his altimeter and temperature gauge were damaged and he was anxious about increasing altitude in these freezing conditions. From the alpine school he telephoned his base requesting spare instruments to be delivered and fitted immediately.

The children viewed the repairs with enthusiasm, especially when they were taken in groups for an unforgettable flight before the pilot's final departure.

GRADED SPELLING TEST

(ii)

ON Will you put the kettle *on*?

HOT The water is *hot*.

CUP Will you have another *cup*?

VAN The furniture came in a *van*.

JAM Do you like sandwiches made of *jam*?

LOST The dog was *lost*.

SIT Where will you *sit*?

PLAN I have a good *plan*.

MUD Their shoes were covered with *mud*.

BEG If the dog wants a biscuit it will *beg*.

THE *The* boy is here.

GO When will you *go*?

FOR It is not *for* me.

SO He went *so* quickly.

ME Please give it to *me*.

ARE They *are* here.

OF The father *of* the boy.

DO What will you *do*?

WHO *Who* are you?

HERE Put it *here*.

SHIP We went in a *ship*.

FOOD I must buy *food*.

FIRE Light the *fire*.

THIN The man was tall and *thin*.

DATE What is the *date*?

CHOP The butcher will *chop* the meat.

SEEM It does not *seem* like winter.

DART The boy threw a *dart*.

LOUD His voice was *loud*.

FORM What *form* are you in?
The children sat on a *form*.

EYE Shut your *eye*.

FIGHT The boy will *fight*.

FRIEND He is my *friend*.

DONE What have you *done*?

ANY Are there *any* left?

GREAT It was a *great*, big animal.

SURE I am *sure*.

WOMEN The *women* stood and waited.

ANSWER Will you please *answer* my question?

BEAUTIFUL The flowers were *beautiful*.

ORCHESTRA The musicians played in an *orchestra*.

EQUALLY They shared the sweets *equally*.

APPRECIATE I *appreciate* your kindness.

FAMILIAR His face was *familiar*.

ENTHUSIASTIC He was very *enthusiastic*

SIGNATURE He wrote his *signature*.

BREATHE Fresh air is good to *breathe*.

PERMANENT The road is *permanent*.

SUFFICIENT The food is *sufficient*.

SURPLUS These stocks are *surplus*.

CUSTOMARY It is *customary* to shake hands.

ESPECIALLY This is *especially* for you.

MATERIALLY It is not *materially* different.

CEMETERY The *cemetery* was cool and silent.

LEISURE His *leisure* was spent in the garden.

FRATERNALLY He wrote *fraternally* to his friend.

SUCCESSFUL The boy was *successful*.

DEFINITE He made a *definite* promise.

EXHIBITION There was an *exhibition* of work.

APPARATUS The *apparatus* was used in an experiment.

MORTGAGE The man took out a *mortgage* on the house.

EQUIPPED The camp was well *equipped*.

SUBTERRANEAN This is a *subterranean* tunnel.

POLITICIAN The *politician* spoke with ease.

MISCELLANEOUS This is a *miscellaneons* collection of goods.

EXAGGERATE Do not *exaggerate* your claim.

GUARANTEE The new car had a year's *guarantee*.

79

TABLE OF NORMS FOR SPELLING TEST

(Daniels and Diack, 1958) supplemented at upper end by Graded Word Spelling Test (Schonell, 1950) with acknowledgments

Mark	Spelling Age	Mark	Spelling Age	Mark	Spelling Age
0	5.0	14	6.5	28	8.2
1	5.2	15	6.6	29	8.3
2	5.3	16	6.7	30	8.5
3	5.4	17	6.8	31	8.7
4	5.5	18	7.0	32	9.0
5	5.6	19	7.1	33	9.2
6	5.7	20	7.2	34	9.5
7	5.8	21	7.3	35	9.8
8	5.9	22	7.5	36	10.2
9	6.0	23	7.6	37	10.5
10	6.1	24	7.7	38	11.0
11	6.2	25	7.8	39	11.6
12	6.3	26	7.9	40	12.3
13	6.4	27	8.1	47	13.0
				52	13.5
				57	14.0
				62	14.5
				67	15.0

Diagnostic dictations

2nd yr junior (9 yrs)
Mean S.A. = 6.63
Excluding words below 9,
Mean S.A. = 9.57

5+	6+	7+	8+	9+	10+	11+
of	neck	with	hair	frightened	certainly	galloped
he (2)	away	street	own	searched	removed	satisfaction
his (2)	that	safe	said	noisy	bridge	
into	back	now	where	field	dangerous	
the (5)	to	happy	brow	opened		
led	belt	very	give	should		
and (3)	so	gate	dinner	traffic		
him (2)	be	tied	apple	heard		
an	from (2)	raincoat	pockets			
my (3)		you	around			
in		for	dark			
me		saw	horse			
and (2)		little	behind			
of (2)		shaggy	turned			
it		down	trotting			
as		walking	sound			
a		was (3)				
I (9)		one				
day						

3rd yr junior (10 yrs)
Mean S.A. = 7.4
Excluding words below 9,
Mean S.A. = 10y

5+	6+	7+	8+	9+	10+	11+	12+
bed	had	left	round	earth	regained	comfortable	actually
an	sank	never	what	dodged	spacecraft	destination	scarcely
we (2)	been	down	sight	edge	accident	height	
us	must	have	about	knife	avoid	relief	
and (2)	away	when	wonder	spinning	whistling	skilfully	
of (3)	we	out (2)	stars	caught	flying	saucer	
to (3)	had	was	beneath	glowed	type	helicopter	
the (7)	saying	of	lights	above	surface		
I (3)	me	were	before	scrambled	beginning		
in	my (3)	into	new	would	city		
a (2)		you	enjoy	friend	track suit		
		woke	might		trial run		
		one					
		late					

81

Diagnostic dictations contd.

4th yr junior (11 yrs)
Mean S.A. = 8.6y
Excluding words
below 9,
Mean S.A. = 10.83y

5+	6+	7+	8+	9+	10+	11+	12+	13+	14+
an	be	they	before	repairs	final	groups	enthusiasm	departure	gauge
he (2)	to	when	flight	fitted	telephoned	viewed	immediately	unforgettable	precision
and (3)	that	these	children (2)	spare	freezing	delivered	requesting	especially	
his (2)	its	were (2)	base	damaged	increasing	instruments	anxious	temperature	
in (3)	from (2)	who	school	pilot('s)	explained	conditions	altimeter	approaching	
the (9)		ever	alpine	surrounded	surface	altitude	machine		
a (2)		with (2)	about	scraping	mountainous	region	designed		
		down	without	rough	circling	aeroplane	distinguished		
		they	shape	touched	recently	gradually	peculiar		
		was (2)		above	valley				
					southern				

enthusiasm

DICTATION FOR 2nd YEAR CHILDREN
analysed according to Burroughs (1957)

75 words

1st 500	2nd 300	3rd 500	4th 500	Used by 4 or fewer children	Not included in B'ham list
	frightened	traffic	led	trot(ting)	searched
	heard	galloped	sound	removed	certainly
	should		dangerous	safe	shaggy
	noisy				satisfaction
	behind				
	around				
	pockets				
	own				
	street				
	happy				
	tied				
	neck				
	belt				

DICTATION FOR 3rd YEAR CHILDREN
analysed according to NZCER frequency levels

59 words

1	2	3	4	5	6	7	not occurring in frequency lists
	left	earth	sight	accident	comfortable	spinning	actually
	caught	round	wonder	whistling	sank	distinction	regained
	lights	flying		saucer	height	beneath	spacecraft
		knife		type			relief
		beginning		surface			avoid
		above		edge			skilfully
		stars		track			dodged
		city		suit			glowed
		enjoy					scrambled
		woke					scarcely
		late					helicopter
							trial run

83

Frequency Levels (NZCER) for words occurring in *Dictation 3* (4th year)

1	2	3	4	5	6	7	(outside lists)
a	aeroplane	above	southern	circling	shape	mountainous	peculiar
was	without	telephoned	valley	machine	surrounded	damaged	approaching
from	ever	groups	region	touched	pilot	increasing	gradually
the	taken		lease	rough	explained	conditions	distinguished
they			viewed	surface	temperature	spare	recently
a			especially	freezing	anxious	instruments	designed
the				fitted	immediately	delivered	precision
down				final	pilot's	flight	scaping
with							altimeter
in							gauge
the							altitude
its							alpine
the							requesting
children							repairs
the							enthusiasm
who							unforgettable
that							departure
his							
and							
were							
and							
he							
was							
about							
in							
these							
from							
the							
school							
he							
his							
to							
be							
and							
the							
children							
the							
with							
when							
they							
were							
in							
for							
an							
before							
the							
46%	4%	3%	6%	8%	8%	8%	17%

	Omissions & Contractions		Insertions		Transpositions		Doubling		Substitution Letter		Substitution Syllable		Faulty Auditory Perception	Homophones	Perseveration	Unclassified Errors
	L	S	L	S	Inversion of Letter	Transposition of Syllable	Single for Double	Double for Single	Consonant	Vowel	Reasonable phonic alternative	Phonic alternative not conforming to rule				
Dictation																
Graded Spelling Test																

85

Questionnaire to teachers of third year Primary School children in the City.

1. Do you teach spelling
   (*a*) from word lists, e.g., Schonell's 'Essential Spelling List'?
   (*b*) from lists you have made up yourself?
   (*c*) from words the children ask for in the course of their free writing?

2. Do you test words
   daily?
   weekly?
   individually?
   in groups?
   as a class?

3. How do children deal with spelling corrections?

4. Do you advise children to try the word first before asking or looking it up?

During the week beginning March 1st, 1965, would you please note:

(A) The amount of time spent each day on actual spelling instruction.
   (to include learning of lists by children
         testing of words
         any incidental teaching of rules
         giving of examples, etc.)

(B) The amount of time spent on free writing.
   i.e., composition
         diary
         description or recording of activities
         (not notes taken from reference books or records in note form)

		Monday March 1	Tuesday March 2	Wednesday March 3	Thursday March 4	Friday March 5
	Lists					
Spelling	Instruction					
	Testing					
Free Writing						

Comments on how you think spelling should be taught would be very much welcomed.

CHILDREN'S WRITING

School:

Class:

Teacher:

Please would you underline which of the following pairs you think is the more important in children's creative writing.

Speed and quantity of output	Neat and pleasant handwriting
Accurate spelling	Correct grammar and punctuation
Lively, vivid writing	Speed and quantity of output
Neat and pleasant handwriting	Accurate spelling
Correct grammar and punctuation	Lively vivid writing
Speed and quantity of output	Correct grammar and punctuation
Lively, vivid writing	Neat and pleasant handwriting
Accurate spelling	Lively, vivid writing
Correct grammar and punctuation	Neat and pleasant handwriting
Speed and quantity of output	Accurate spelling

Please would you underline which of the following describes your *most usual* practice:

The children give in their composition books for marking.
I mark the children's books as they write.
The children write in pencil and rub out their mistakes as I correct them.
The children formally learn the words they have asked for in their dictionaries or word books.
The children formally learn word lists from Schonell's or some such list.
The children learn word lists I make up.
The children do not formally learn lists.

I encourage them to write interesting compositions and not bother about spelling or punctuation.

I try as far as possible to get correct spelling and punctuation.

APPENDIX B

 (i) Summary of items of information obtained: Child Variable
 (ii) Summary of items of information obtained: Teaching variable
 (iii) Means and Variances of attainment (Child Variable)
 (iv) Means and Variances of percentage progress (Child Variable)
 (v) Comparison of means and variances of spelling attainment, actual progress and percentage progress according to grades of verbal intelligence.

(i)

SUMMARY OF ITEMS OF INFORMATION OBTAINED

Child Variable

Sex	
School	
Term of year born:	September to December
	January to April
	May to August
Socio-economic status:	1 to 5. Registrar-General's classification
Place in family:	Only child
	Eldest
	Youngest
	Middle
Size of family:	Number of children
Handedness (writing)	
Visual defect:	Children with spectacles
Auditory defect:	Children having received audiometric testing other than as screening measure
Speed of handwriting:	Grades 1. 8 letters completed in 10 seconds
	2. 5 to 8 letters completed in 10 seconds
	3. 4 or fewer letters completed in 10 seconds
Carefulness:	Grades 1. Handwriting well-formed
	2. Legible but casual
	3. Barely legible, or very casual, uncontrolled or messy
11+ selection	
Primary verbal test:	Mean of N.F.E.R. P.V.1 and P.V.3
Spelling score:	Test 11 from Standard Reading Tests, Daniels and Diack at 9+, 10+ and 11+ supplemented by Schonell Spelling Test
Actual spelling progress:	9 to 10, 10 to 11, 9 to 11
Percentage spelling progress	
Visual perception of word form:	Grades 1. Whole word correct
	2. 5 letters in correct order
	3. 4 or fewer letters in correct order or 5 to 8 letters out of sequence
Auditory perception:	Grade 1. No errors of auditory perception throughout
	Grade 2. One error of faulty auditory perception
	Grade 3. More than one error of faulty auditory perception; words omitted or substituted

88

<table>
<tr><td>Rational approach:</td><td>Grade 1.</td><td>All words correct or more reasonable alternatives than unreasonable</td></tr>
<tr><td></td><td>Grade 2.</td><td>Equal number of reasonable and unreasonable alternatives</td></tr>
<tr><td></td><td>Grade 3.</td><td>More unreasonable than reasonable alternatives</td></tr>
</table>

By reasonable alternative is meant conformity with rule or precedent, e.g., certainly spelt 'sur' (surface)

'cir' (circle)

'sir' but not 'saer'

Again, pocits (pockets) was not considered reasonable

Teacher's grade in third year:	1 to 5
Teacher's grade in fourth year:	1 to 5
Mean of teachers' grades for two years:	1 to 5
Streamed/unstreamed class	

(ii)
SUMMARY OF ITEMS OF INFORMATION OBTAINED

Teaching Variable

Sex
School
Mean socio-economic status of children in each class (5 point scale)
Year :   2, 2.5, 3, 3.5, 4.
Stream
Attitudes to what is important in creative writing :

Vividness
Output
Spelling
Grammar and Punctuation
Handwriting

Consistency of attitude obtained from paired comparisons between the items
Grades of technical skill according to indices :

Consistency of policy, regular and systematic testing, rational marking practice and exacting of rational correction practice.

Methodology :   Teaching by lists, if so the origin of these lists.

Time spent on list learning, instruction
Total time spent on spelling
Total time spent on creative writing
'Corrections' practice
'Trying out' of words

Testing practice : Time spent, frequency, organization.
Mean actual progress in spelling of class during year.
Mean percentage progress in spelling of class during year.

G

ACTUAL SPELLING ATTAINMENT AT 9 YEARS

Mean score   29.75

Related to: S.D.   9.35

S.E.S.

	1	2	3	4	5
Number of cases	62	186	315	200	83
Means	36.69	33.52	30.43	25.67	23.4
Variances	15.00	40.03	63.88	117.72	117.71

Place in family

	Only	Eldest	Youngest	Middle
Number of cases	75	224	282	265
Means	31.92	30.72	30.17	27.88
Variances	49.80	77.66	85.50	103.62

Handedness

	Lefthanded	Righthanded
Number of cases	100	746
Means	26.47	30.19
Variances	5.24	83.59

Visual defect

	Spectacles worn	Vision normal
Number of cases	91	755
Means	31.58	29.53
Variances	74.65	88.68

Auditory defect

	Auditory defect suspected	Hearing normal
Number of cases	61	785
Means	27.82	29.91
Variances	18.15	84.93

Speed of handwriting

	Swift	Average	Slow
Number of cases	540	223	83
Means	33.95	23.82	18.42
Variances	35.15	85.42	97.56

Carefulness

	Writing carefully formed	Legible but casual	Barely legible or very casual
Number of cases	123	532	191
Means	36.65	31.73	19.88
Variances	11.06	53.24	93.58

Fluency

	Grades	A	B	C	D	E
Number of cases		78	194	280	170	124
Means		37.72	35.57	31.92	25.72	16.31
Variances		4.44	16.97	42.89	61.9	80.25

Subsequent 11+

	Selection	for	Secondary Modern	Grammar Schools
Number of cases			639	207
Means			27.29	37.37
Variances			88.96	6.14

Visual perception of word form

	Good	Average	Poor
Number of cases	290	287	269
Means	36.63	31.36	20.63
Variances	8.27	40.41	86.20

Auditory perception

	Good	Average	Poor
Number of cases	278	207	361
Means	36.47	33.2	22.61
Variances	10.20	26.87	89.34

Rational approach

	Rational	Irrational
Number of cases	410	436
Means	35.88	23.99
Variances	15.25	86.97

Streaming

	Unstreamed School	Streamed School
Number of cases	206	640
Means	31.74	29.12
Variances	70.41	91.41

Subsequent ability to transfer letter sequences at 11

	Capable	Incapable
Number of cases	369	477
Means	36.05	24.88
Variances	12.24	91.28

PERCENTAGE SPELLING PROGRESS

Related to:

S.E.S.

	1	2	3	4	5
Number of cases	62	186	315	200	83
Means	24.24	28.34	31.78	51.34	52.60
Variances	1.8	8.2	10.7		

Place in family

	Only	Eldest	Youngest	Middle
Number of cases	75	224	282	265
Means	39.17	37.3	35.81	37.83
Variances	30.14	28.9	21.78	18.96

Handedness

	Lefthanded	Righthanded
Number of cases	100	746
Means	53.44	34.95
Variances	24.23	19.61

Visual defect

	Spectacles worn	Vision normal
Number of cases	91	755
Means	38.65	36.96
Variances	33.43	32.09

Auditory defect

	Auditory defect suspected	Hearing normal
Number of cases	61	785
Means	48.02	36.29
Variances	73.14	29.01

Speed of handwriting

	Swift	Average	Slow
Number of cases	540	223	83
Means	24.89	51.13	79.31
Variances	3.89	36.53	74.15

Carefulness

	Writing carefully formed	Legible but casual	Barely legible or very casual
Number of cases	123	532	191
Means	23.45	28.65	69.49
Variances	1.73	12.58	93.19

Fluency

	Grades	A	B	C	D	E
Number of cases		78	194	280	170	124
Means		29.3	23.23	27.85	36.08	86.23
Variances		2.3	1.66	11.04	11.02	147.25

11+ selection

	for	Secondary Modern	Grammar Schools
Number of cases		639	207
Means		40.42	27
Variances		41.61	1.83

Visual perception of word form

	Good	Average	Poor
Number of cases	290	287	269
Means	23.49	24.88	64.94
Variances	1.9	5.11	82.64

Auditory perception

	Good	Average	Poor
Number of cases	278	207	361
Means	23.45	21.18	56.83
Variances	1.96	2.12	66.06

Rational approach

	Rational	Irrational
Number of cases	410	436
Means	22.42	50.78
Variances	1.74	57.95

Streaming

	Unstreamed School	Streamed School
Number of cases	206	640
Means	30.21	39.37
Variances	5.24	30.21

Mean Teacher's Grade

	A	B	C	D	E
Number of cases	74	145	419	179	29
Means	28.74	37.83	40.75	34.74	17.76
Variances	2.26	17.01	30.23	65.25	4.04

Transfer of letter sequences at 11

	Capable	Incapable
Number of cases	369	477
Means	23.2	47.96
Variances	1.8	52.07

COMPARISON OF MEANS AND VARIANCES OF SPELLING ATTAINMENT, ACTUAL PROGRESS AND PERCENTAGE PROGRESS ACCORDING TO GRADES OF VERBAL INTELLIGENCE

Spelling attainment at 9 years

	Verbal intelligence					
	Lowest					*Highest*
Number of cases	25	183	304	239	88	7
Means	12.24	19.60	30.21	35.53	37.79	39.43
Variances	28.11	72.26	52.04	11.89	6.44	0.62

Actual spelling progress from 9 to 11 years

Means	7.44	8.93	6.82	7.5	12.15	14.43
Variances	29.76	26.27	14.0	16.43	29.14	32.62

Percentage spelling progress

Means	100.44	67.88	27.64	21.11	31.68	36.14
Variances	374.43	59.61	10.51	1.51	1.96	2.03

APPENDIX C

  (i)   Analysis of the spelling of the word 'saucer'
 (ii)   Examples of children's spelling
(iii) Examples of teachers' comments

APPENDIX C :　　　　　　　　　　　(i)

The spelling, by 967 ten year old children, of the word 'saucer' (total number 988)*

Correct　　　462
Incorrect　　505
*Omitted by　21

Alternatives

sauser	67	seser ⎫	sarter	scoue	sosed
sorser	23	soer	sary	scour	sosar
suacer	23	sora	sascaue	scouse	sosiar
sacer	20	sorsa	sasger	scuace	sosre
sorcer	18	sos	sasere	scuarcer	sou
soser ⎫		sose ⎬ 2	sasher	scuccer	sourcer
soucer ⎬ 11		sosr	satard	scare	sourses
sucer ⎭		suar	saucere	scuser	sout
suser	10	sus	saucor	senrd	sowew
sawser	9	susar	saucing	serner	space
sarser ⎫		suse ⎭	saucher	sem	spanger
sarcer			saucter	ses	spcae
sacar ⎬ 8			saue	sesaur	spienace
sauce		carser	saues	sharser	sres
scaucer ⎭		causer	saught	shasers	slous
souser	7	chocer	saura	shose	suace
sauer ⎫ 5		cor	saurse	shower	suarser
sause ⎬		corroce	saus	shure	suaser
caucer ⎫		corser	sauscer	sice	sucar
sawer		curser	sausery	sinder	succer
socer		eswas	sausir	sined	sucase
sorer ⎬ 4		sacar	sausue	slart	suce
surcer		sacca	sausur	sloy	sucger
surser		saccer	savcr	smory	suecher
scauer		sacerer	sawers	soc	sueer
saser ⎬		sacir	sawur	socp	sucur
saurcer		sacuere	sayser	splorns	sud
saurser		sacuers	seacar	soolle	suger
scarcer ⎬ 3		saer	scace	sooser	suier
suscer		saeucng	searces	sooucer	sumser
suarcer		sancer	scaresere	sor	suorser
sausar ⎭		saose	scarser	sore	surage
cacer ⎫		sarce	scaser	sorcr	surce
sauccer		sarear	scasur	sororr	surer
sarsar		sare	scauser	sors	sureer
saursar ⎬ 2		saresir	scocer	sorsar	sursar
scar		sari	scoors	sorscur	sursur
scare		sarig	scorceri	sorb	surts
scaser		saroer	scoser	sorur	susare
scorer		sarry	scoua	sorus	susas
sercer ⎭		sarses	scoucel	sosa	sues
					sye
					syer

95

Samples of children's spelling

Examples of 1. Substitutions   Reasonable phonic alternative :
'tighed' for 'tied'
'gait' for 'gate'
'kneck' for 'neck'
Phonic alternative not conforming to rule :
'fiteurned' for 'frightened'

2. Faulty auditory
perception :   'chroting' for 'trotting'
3. Homophones : 'tide' for 'tied'
4. Perseveration : 'flagishfashon' for 'flagrancy' (in test for visual perception for word form, having recently written 'satisefachen' for 'satisfaction').

One lively interjection occurred where a child digressed in the middle of the diagnostic dictation (9 years) to write 'trotting, a trotting horse, blue eyes champion runner'!

Examples of children with contrasting grades of visual and auditory perception

1. *School A :*   Child 28 : Girl careful, methodical and attentive ; writes every word.
Auditory perception efficient (grade 1) because dependent on attention.
Visual perception of word form poor (grade 3) : 'Flagury' for 'Flagrancy'.
Visual perception of word form, where poor very influential. This child's progress through the two years is erratic, improving and then deteriorating.

2. *School B :*   Child 99 : Girl. Visual perception good (grade 1).
Auditory perception poor (grade 3) (10 omissions) (3 words added.) Very poor attention—personality factor ? Deteriorates in spelling through the two years.

3. *School C :*   Child 153 : Boy. Visual perception good (grade 1).
Auditory perception poor (grade 3).
Omits 1 word ; adds 1 and substitutes 1.
Writes 'pear' for 'hair'
'a' for 'an'
'sick' for 'safe'
'tracky' for 'traffic'.
Percentage improvement in two years : 40%

Examples of comments made by teachers in the sample on the teaching of spelling

School	Stream	
A	A	Choice of words should arise from real need, related to work in progress.
B	A	I have grave doubts whether you can teach spelling at all in a direct and lasting way, e.g., many children get full marks in a weekly test but do very badly in a comprehensive end of year examination. I feel sure that the prime factor in spelling ability is the quantity of reading accomplished over the years by a child and especially in boys is not so greatly connected with writing ability.
		Vital to keep spelling standards before children.
B	B	Short periods of formal teaching or testing necessary with all children. A hope that they will learn whilst reading applies only to a few.
		The drill gets the better ones into the habit of looking at words.
M	A	Write freely whether they can spell it or not. I do not know whether I am right to do no list learning, perhaps your tests will give some answer to this. I do think an excitement with words and many needs to use words in which the child is really interested and personally involved, do seem important.
L	A	I feel children, even the brightest, can be lazy where spelling is concerned. At the beginning of the year I would personally correct any important word in their free writing. I felt a situation developed where the child became carefree and careless with spelling since he felt that his errors would be corrected by me and that was the end of the matter.
		Since Christmas I have underlined words that should be known and put a cross over them. The child then finds the word in his dictionary and writes it in his word book which I supervise. The extra labour involved by the child has made him think more before writing and spelling, especially in free writing, has improved.
		This has not limited the quality of the free writing.
K	B	I feel that spelling lists include many words that have no immediate impact—perhaps no value.
O		Providing that there is sufficient enrichment in the form of the spoken and the read word (and providing that this is sufficiently active, emotional and meaningful) there would seem no need to 'teach' spelling in a formal way. I would go further. I often think that an over elaborate system of 'analysing' English is a barrier to the free creative development of the child, causing at its extreme a complete lack of faith in the child's own potential. In other words 'bad spellers' can still be taught to communicate.
C	A	Spelling should be taught informally as much as possible with encouragement and the use of dictionaries.
C	B	There can be no hard and fast rules. The approach to spell depends upon the child. The less able children tend to need 'word-drill' more than the highly intelligent children who can learn quite naturally.
E	A	The headteacher is of the view that the spelling in the school is very poor and recommends a more formal approach to the teaching of the subject.
E	B	Children write in pencil without asking for any words at all. They read their work to the class. Then they look at their work and underline any word which they think is not correctly spelt. This is rubbed out and they discover how they should have spelt the word, by looking in dictionaries, by asking each other, by asking me. Many can find all their own mistakes

97

COMBINATIONS OF PREDICTIVE VARIABLES

FREQUENCY TABLE OF COMBINATIONS OF VARIABLES

	11	12	13	(Σ)		01	02	03	(Σ)	(Σ)
11	66	24	3	93	11	8	3	4	15	108
12	153	85	11	249	12	35	64	40	139	388
13	9	4	3	16	13		14	14	28	44
(Σ):	228	113	17	358		43	81	58	182	540
	11	12	13			01	02	03		
21	2	2	2	6	21		3	2	5	11
22	6	22	10	38	22	2	29	45	76	114
23		6	8	14	23	5	77	62	84	98
(Σ):	8	30	20	58		7	49	109	165	223
	11	12	13			01	02	03		
31	1		1	2	31			1	1	3
32	1	3	2	6	32	1	5	17	23	29
33		1	2	3	33		6	42	48	41
(Σ):	2	4	5	11		1	11	60	72	83
(Σ):	238	147	42	427		51	141	227	419	846 (Σ)

Sample size 846

Variables

1 Speed   Grades: 1.2.3.
2 Carefulness   Grades: 1.2.3.
3 Verbal intelligence: 0.1. (below 7 above median 101)
4 Visual perception of word form Grades: 1.2.3.

MEANS

	11	12	13		01	02	03	
11	48.77	44.04	41.33	11	42.12	42.33	39.5	43.01
12	46.24	41.26	38.73	12	39.8	37.64	33.02	39.45
13	45.77	39.75	37.0	13		32.43	25.86	36.16
	11	12	13		01	02	03	
21	45.5	42.0	35.5	21		32.00	34.0	37.8
22	41.33	40.73	37.4	22	38.5	34.89	29.93	37.13
23		37.83	37.5	23	37.4	32.41	25.32	34.09
	11	12	13		01	02	03	
31	36.0		39.0	31			38.0	37.66
32	40.0	34.66	45.0	32	41.0	30.8	25.18	36.11
33		42.0	19.0	33		30.0	23.28	28.57
	43.37	40.32	36.72		39.76	34.06	30.45	

Bibliography

AHLSTROM, K. G. (1964). *Studies of Spelling*. Institute of Education, Uppsala University.

ANDERSON, I. H. (1965). *Comparisons of the Reading and Spelling Achievements and Quality of Handwriting of Groups of English, Scottish and American Children*. University of Michigan.

ANDREWS, R. (1964). Research Study No. 9. University of Queensland Papers, Faculty of Education, i, No. 4.

ARVIDSON, G. L. (1963). *Learning to Spell*. Wheaton.

AYRES, L. P. (1913). *The Spelling Vocabularies of Personal and Business Letters*. Russell Sage Foundation, New York.

BELTRAMO, L. (1954). *An Alphabetical Approach to the Teaching of Reading in Grade One*. State University of Iowa. Dissertation Abstracts, 14, 2290.

BENNETT, D. M. (1967). *New Methods and Materials in Spelling. A Critical Analysis*. Australian Council for Educational Research.

BIXLER, H. (1940). *The Standard Elementary Spelling Scale*. Turner E. Smith & Co., Atlanta.

BREED, F. S. (1925). 'What Words Should Children Be Taught to Spell?' *Elementary School Journal*, xxvi, 118–131, 202–214, 292–306.

BRUNER, J. S. and HARCOURT, R. A. F. (1953). *Going Beyond the Information Given*. Unpublished manuscript.

BRUNER, J. S., *et al.* (1966). *Studies in Cognitive Growth*. Wiley.

BURROUGHS, G. E. R. (1957). *A Study of the Vocabulary of Young Children*. Oliver and Boyd.

BURT, C. (1937). *The Backward Child*. University of London Press.

CLARK, M. M. (1957). *Lefthandedness*. University of London Press.

CLARKE, M. R. B. (1966). *Maximum Likelihood and Varimax Rotation Factor Analysis*. University of London Institute of Computer Science.

COOK, W. A. and O'SHEA, M. V. (1914). *The Child and His Spelling*. Bobbs-Merrell, Indianapolis.

CORNMAN, O. P. (1902). *Spelling in the Elemetary School*, Ginn, Boston.

CRONBACH, L. J. (1954). *Educational Psychology*, Harcourt Brace, New York.

DANIELS, J. G. and DIACK, H. (1958). *The Standard Reading Tests*, Chattow and Windus.

DIACK, H. (1960). *Reading and the Psychology of Perception*. Peter Skinner Publishing Ltd.

EDWARDS, R. P. A. and GIBBON, V. (1964). *Words Your Children Use*. Burke, London.

EFROYMSON, M. A. (1962). 'Stepwise Regression.' *Mathematical Methods for Digital Computers*. ed. Ralston & Wilf, Wiley.

ELDRIDGE, R. C. (1911). *Six Thousand Common English Words*. The Clement Press, Buffalo.

EWING, A. (1965). *A Scottish Viewpoint*. Appendix to Anderson, I. H. (1965) (see above).

FENDRICK, P. (1935). *Visual Characteristics of Poor Readers*. Contributions to Education, No. 656. New York Bureau of Publications.

FERNALD, G. M. (1943). *Remedial Techniques in Basic School Subjects*. McGraw-Hill, New York.

FITZGERALD, J. A. (1953). 'The Teaching of Spelling.' *Elementary English*, xxx, 79–85.

FORAN, T. G. (1934). *The Psychology and Teaching of Spelling*. Catholic Education Press, Washington, D.C.

FREYBERG, P. S. (1960). *Teaching Spelling to Juniors*. Macmillan.

FREYBERG, P. S. (1964). 'A Comparison of Two Approaches to the Teaching of Spelling.' *British Journal of Educational Psychology*, xxiv, 178–186.

FRIES, C. C. (1962). *Linguistics and Reading*. Holt, Rinehart and Winston.

FULTON, M. J. (1914). 'An Experiment in Teaching Spelling.' *Pedagogical Seminary*, xxi, 287–9.

GATES, A. I. (1937). *Spelling Difficulties in 3876 Words*. New York Bureau of Publications, Teachers' College, Columbia University.

GATES, A. I. and RUSSELL, D. H. (1940). *Diagnostic and Remedial Spelling Manual*. New York Bureau of Publications, Teachers' College, Columbia University.

GIBSON, E. J. (1965). 'Learning to Read.' *Science*, Vol. 148.

GILBERT, L. C. (1932a). 'An Experimental Investigation of a Flash-Card Method of Teaching Spelling.' *Elementary School Journal*, xxxii, 337–351.

GILBERT, L. C. (1932b). 'An Experimental Investigation of Eye-Movements in Learning to Spell Words.' *Psychological Monograph*, xliii, 3.

GILBERT, L. C. (1935). 'Study of the Effect of Reading on Spelling.' *Journal of Educational Research*, xxviii, 570–576.

GILBERT, L. C. and GILBERT, D. W. (1942). 'Training for Speed and Accuracy of Visual Perception in Learning to Spell.' *California University Publications in Education*, VII No. 5, 351–426.

GILL, E. J. (1912). 'The Teaching of Spelling.' *Journal of Experimental Pedagogy*, I, 310–319.

GOSS, J. E. (1959). 'Analysis of Accuracy of Spelling in Written Compositions of Elementary School Children and the Effects of Proofreading Emphasis upon Accuracy.' Doctor's Thesis. Norman University of Oklahoma. Cit De Boer, J. J. (1961). 'Composition, Handwriting and Spelling.' *Review of Educational Research*, xxxi, 2, 161–172.

GREENE, H. A. (1954). *The New Iowa Spelling Scale*. State University of Iowa, Bureau of Educational Research and Service.

GROFF, P. J. (1961). 'The New Iowa Spelling Scale: How Phonetic is it?' *Elementary School Journal*, lxii, 46–49.

HANNA, P. R. and HANNA, J. S. (1965). 'Application of Linguistics and Psychological Cues to the Spelling Course of Study.' *Elementary English*, xlii, 7, 753–759.

HANNA, P. R. and MOORE, J. T. (1953). 'Spelling from Spoken Word to Written Symbol.' *Elementary School Journal*, liii, 329–337.

HARTMANN, G. W. (1931). 'The Relative Influence of Visual and Auditory Factors in Spelling Ability.' *Journal of Educational Psychology*, xxii, 9, 691–699.

HEBB, D. O. (1968). *Psychological Review*, lxxv, 6, 466–477.

HIGLEY, B. R. and HIGLEY, B. M. (1936). 'An Effective Method of Learning to Spell.' *Educational Research Bulletin*, xv, 9, Columbus-Ohio State University.

HILDERBRANDT, E. (1923). 'The Psychological Analysis of Spelling.' *Pedagogical Seminary*, xxx, 371–381.

HILDRETH, G. H. (1953). 'Inter-Grade Comparisons of Word Frequencies in Children's Writing'. *Journal of Educational Pscychology*, xliv, 7, 429–435.

HILDRETH, G. H. (1956). *Teaching Spelling*. Henry Holt, New York.

HODGES, R. E. and RUDORF, E. H. (1965). 'Linguistic Clues in Teaching Spelling'. *Elementary English*, xliii, 5, 527–533.

HOLMES, J. A. (1959). 'Personality and Spelling Ability'. *University of California Publications in Education*, xii, 4, 213–292.

HORN, E. (1919). 'Principles of Teaching Spelling as Derived from Scientific Investigation.' *National Society for the Study of Education 18th Year Book, Part II*, Bloomington (III.). Public School Publishing Co., 52–77.

HORN, E. (1926). 'A Basic Writing Vocabulary: 10,000 Words Most Commonly Used in Writing'. *Monographs in Education*, 4, University of Iowa.

HORN, E. (1929). 'A Source of Confusion in Spelling'. *Journal of Educational Research*, xix, 47–55.

HORN, E. (1952). *Teaching Spelling* (What Research Says to the Teacher No. 3). Washington National Education Association, 32 pp.

HORN, E. (1960). 'Spelling'. *Encl. of Educational Research*, Macmillan.

HORN, T. D. (1967). 'Handwriting and Spelling'. *Review of Educational Research*, xxxvii, 2.

HOWES, D. H. and SOLOMON, R. L. (1951). 'Visual Duration Threshold as a Function of Word Probablity'. *Journal of Experimental Psychology*, xli, 401–410.

JENSEN, A. R. (1962). 'Spelling Errors and the Serial Position Effect'. *Journal of Educational Psychology*, liii, 105–109.

JOHNSON, L. W. (1950). 'One Hundred Words most often Mis-spelled by Children in the Elementary Grades'. *Journal of Educational Research*, xliv, 154–155.

KUHLMAN, C. (1960). 'Visual Imagery in Children'. Unpublished doctoral dissertation. Harvard University, cit Bruner (1966) (see above).

KYTE, G. C. (1948). 'When Spelling Has Been Mastered in the Elementary School'. *Journal of Educational Research*, xli, 47–53.

LECKY, P. (1945). *Self-consistency, A Theory of Personality*. Island Press, New York.

LESTER, M. (1964). 'Graphemic-phonemic Correspondence as the Basis for Teaching Spelling'. *Elementary English*, xli, 7, 748–752.

LIVINGSTON, A. A. (1961). 'A Study of Spelling Errors'. *Studies of Spelling*. University of London Press.

MACKAY, D. and THOMPSON, B. (1968). 'The Initial Teaching of Reading and Writing'. Paper 3 in *Progress in Linguistics and English Teaching*. Longmans.

MACKINNON, A. R. (1959). *How Do Children Learn to Read?* Copp Clark.

McLEISH, J. (1969). 'Systems, Models, Simulations and Games in Education'. Unpublished paper.

McLEOD, M. E. (1961). 'Rules in the Teaching of Spelling'. *Studies in Spelling*, University of London Press.

McNALLY, J. and MURRAY, W. (1965). *Key Words to Literacy*. School Master Publishing Company.

MARKSHEFFEL, N. D. (1964). 'Composition, Handwriting and Spelling'. *Review of Educational Research*, xxxiv, 2, 182–183.

MASON, G. P. (1961). 'Word Discrimination Drills'. *Journal of Educational Research*, lv, 39–40.

MASTERS, H. V. (1927). *A Study of Spelling Errors*. University of Iowa Studies in Education, iv, 4.

NEW ZEALAND COUNCIL FOR EDUCATIONAL RESEARCH (1963). *Alphabetical Spelling List*, Wheaton.

NISBET, S. D. (1939). 'Non-dictated Spelling Tests.' *British Journal of Educational Psychology*, ix, 29–44.

NISBET, S. D. (1941). 'The Scientific Investigation of Spelling Instruction in Scottish Schools'. *British Journal of Educational Psychology*, xi, 150.

PETERS, M. L. (1967). *Spelling: Caught or Taught?* Students Library of Education, Routledge and Kegan Paul, London.

RADAKAR, L. D. (1963). 'The Effect of Visual Imagery Upon Spelling Performance'. *Journal of Educational Research*, lvi, 370–372.

RAVEN, J. G. (1956). *Coloured Progressive Matrices*, H. K. Lewis.

RICE, J. M. (1897). 'The Futility of the Splling Grind'. *Forum*, xxiii.

RICHMOND, A. E. (1960). 'Children's Spelling Needs and the Implications of Research'. *Journal of Experimental Education*, xxix, 3–21.

RINSLAND, H. D. (1945). *A Basic Writing Vocabulary of Elementary School Children*, Macmillan, New York.

ROY, S. N. (1957). *Some Aspects of Multivariate Analysis*. New York: John Wiley & Sons, Calcutta.

RUSSELL, D. H. (1937). *Characteristics of Good and Poor Spellers.* Contributions to Education No. 727. Bureau of Publications, Columbia Teachers' College.

SCHONELL, F. J. (1932). *Essentials in Teaching and Testing Spelling.* Macmillan.

SCHONELL, F. J. (1942). *Backwardness in the Basic Subjects,* Oliver and Boyd.

SCHONELL, F. J. and F. E. (1950). *Diagnostic and Attainment Testing.* Oliver and Boyd.

SCOTTISH COUNCIL FOR RESEARCH IN EDUCATION (1961). *Studies in Spelling.* University of London Press.

Scottish Pupil's Spelling Book (1955). Parts I–V, and *Teacher's Book.* University of London Press.

SHORT, P. L., and WALTER, W. GREY (1954). 'The Relationship Between Physiological Variables and Stereognosis'. *E.E.G. and Clinical Neurophysiology,* 29–44.

SIEGEL, S. (1956). *Non-Parametric Statistics for the Behavioural Sciences.* McGraw-Hill, New York.

SMITH, J. (1961). *Spelling.* Books I to IV. Cassell.

SPACHE, G. (1940a). 'A Critical Analysis of Various Methods of Classifying Spelling Errors, I'. *Journal of Educational Psychology,* xxxi, 2, 11–134.

SPACHE, G. (1940b). 'Validity and Reliability of the Proposed Classification of Spelling Errors, II'. *Journal of Educational Psychology,* xxxi, 3, 204–214.

SPACHE, G. (1940c). 'The Role of Visual Defects in Spelling and Reading Disabilities'. *American Journal of Orthopsychiatry,* x, 229–237.

SPACHE, G. (1953). Review of 'Gates-Russell Spelling Diagnosis Test' in the *Fourth Mental Measurements Yearbook.* Gryphon Press, New Jersey.

STEWART, C. A. and MACFARLANE SMITH (1959). 'The Alpha Rhythm, Imagery and Spatial and Verbal Abilities'. *Durham Research Review,* 272–286.

THORNDIKE, E. L. and LORGE, I. (1944). *The Teacher's Word Book,* 3rd edition. Bureau of Publications, Teacher's College, Columbia University.

TOWNSEND, A. (1947). 'An Investigation of Certain Relationships of Spelling with Reading and Academic Aptitude'. *Journal of Educational Research,* xl, 465–471.

VALLINS, G. H. Revised by SCRAGG, D. G. (1965). *Spelling.* Deutsch.

VENEZKY, D. and LESTER, M. (1964). 'Graphemic-phonemic Correspondence as the Basis for Teaching Spelling'. *Elementary English,* xli, 7, 748–752, cit Lester M. (1964). (see above).

WALLACH, M. A. (1963). 'Perceptual Recognition of Approximations to English in Relation to Spelling Achievement. *Journal of Educational Psychology,* civ, 57–62.

WALLIN, J. E. W. (1910). 'Has the Drill Become Obsclescent?' *Journal of Educational Psychology,* 200–213.

WASHBURNE, C. (1923). 'A Spelling Curriculum Based on Research'. *Elementary School Journal,* xxiii, 751–762.

WATSON, A. (1935). *Experimental Studies in the Psychology and Pedagogy of Spelling.* Contributions to Education, No. 638, Teachers' College, Columbia University.

WHEAT, L. B. (1932). 'Four Spelling Rules'. *Elementary School Journal,* xxxii, 697–706.